GADAMER: A GU
THE PERPLEXED

THE GUIDES FOR THE PERPLEXED SERIES

GADAMER: A GUIDE FOR THE PERPLEXED

CHRIS LAWN

continuum
LONDON • NEW YORK

CONTINUUM International Publishing Group
The Tower Building
11 York Road
London SE1 7NX

80 Maiden Lane
Suite 704
New York
NY 10038

First published 2006
www.continuumbooks.com

British Library Cataloguing-in-Publication Data
A catalogue record for this book is available from the British Library.

ISBN: 0-8264-8461-1 (hardback)   0-8264-8462-X (paperback)

Library of Congress Cataloging-in-Publication Data
A catalog record for this book is available from the Library of Congress.

Typeset by Servis Filmsetting Ltd, Manchester
Printed and bound in Great Britain by
Ashford Colour Press Ltd, Gosport, Hampshire

CONTENTS

CONTENTS

ABBREVIATION

TM   *Truth and Method* (1989). Second revised edition, revised
translation by J. Weinsheimer and D. G. Marshall, London:
Sheed & Ward.

PREFACE

The proposal for this work came from Hywel Evans, former commissioning editor in philosophy for Continuum, and I wish to thank him for inviting me to contribute to the series. The idea for the Guides for the Perplexed, as I understand it, is to elucidate the complex and difficult philosophical ideas of important thinkers. I hope I have been faithful to this brief. Most studies on Gadamer tend to focus exclusively upon his major work *Truth and Method* (*TM*, 1989). This present study has sought to go further by tracing the developments in Gadamer's thought over the 40 years or so after the first publication of *Truth and Method*. I am aware that Gadamer is responsible for a large body of studies on classical thought. His innovative hermeneutical studies, particularly of Plato and Aristotle, are not given the treatment they deserve here, being at best mentioned in passing.

I have sought to present the key ideas and themes in Hans-Georg Gadamer's work and explain them in non-technical terms. Although Gadamer often assumes a detailed knowledge of the history of philosophy he is wilfully non-technical, steering clear of the kind of philosophy that revels in the logic of fine distinctions. This is for a variety of reasons. Firstly, he stands within in an academic tradition that is not always familiar to those working in the Anglo-American analytic philosophical mainstream. I have been conscious of this and sought to provide the necessary background and, further, make Gadamer relevant to ideas and movements beyond his own terms of reference, that is, the German intellectual tradition.

Secondly, Gadamer is initially difficult to place because his work is not easily classifiable and his intellectual project seems so wide-ranging and general.

In conventional philosophical terms he is not doing metaphysics or ethics or political philosophy and yet he manages to work in such a way as to make his philosophical hermeneutics relevant to all of these activities and much more besides. Certainly his project is philosophical but it extends well beyond the often-narrow range of many contemporary philosophers. Gadamer seeks to make sense of human understanding as a philosophical, historical and cultural phenomenon. He also, especially in his later works, brings out the hermeneutical dimension to all human activities and is able to offer a measure of critique.

One might see Gadamer as one of the last of those polymath European intellectuals, gifted with living and dead languages, and as conversant with developments in abstract art as he was knowledgeable about anthropology, linguistics and philosophy. Like Richard Rorty's 'post-philosophical' intellectuals, Gadamer's field of vision for intellectual curiosity was extensive and his central idea that all understanding is essentially dialogue is best achieved when the confines of narrow specialism are no longer appropriate and philosophical, literary, scientific, ideas rub shoulders with relative ease.

Finally, Gadamer is difficult because his terminology whilst not technical is tricky, being frequently suggestive, elusive and without precision. This, I suggest, is no accident as his work is anxious to keep open the interpretive space upon which his hermeneutics resolutely concentrates.

Many colleagues, students and friends have stimulated my interest in Gadamer over the years. A special debt of gratitude is owed to my colleague and friend Louise Campbell who obligingly read and commented upon the chapter on aesthetics, although any infelicities and misinterpretations are entirely my own. Mary Fox, Jeff Lambert, Joby Hennessy, Angus Mitchell and Treasa Campbell, without realizing it, did me a favour by forcing me to explain *Truth and Method* and the importance of Gadamer: I am not sure that I succeeded but the attempt was productive as the result is this book. In conclusion I want to thank Margaret for her forbearance and Omar and Polly for constant companionship.

Chris Lawn
Desert Cross, Enniskeane, Co. Cork, Ireland
September 2005
clawn@eircom.net

INTRODUCTION

GADAMER IN A NUTSHELL

How would one describe a philosopher's achievement in a few brief sentences? In *Great Thinkers A–Z* I rose to this challenge and wrote the entry on Gadamer. The only instruction from the editors was that the piece could not be more than 800 words so it had to be short and concise. This is what I wrote:

Since Descartes, modern philosophy regarded correct *method* as a route to absolute certainty. Armed with a rational procedure, human thought becomes equal to natural science in replacing the dark forces of tradition with objective truth. The work of Hans-Georg Gadamer (1900–2002) contests this optimistic account of modernity, especially in the major work *Truth and Method* (1960). Gadamer starts by re-valuing the idea of tradition – from which Enlightenment thought distanced itself – claiming that 'tradition' and 'reason' cannot be so easily teased apart. For Gadamer, tradition cannot be an object of 'pure' rational enquiry. The idea that we can step outside our own cultural reference points to embrace timeless truth is a demonstrable fiction of modernist thought.

Gadamer relates his idea of 'tradition' to a reworked notion of 'prejudice', which he understands as pre-judice or *pre*-judgement, in other words as that which makes *any* kind of discrimination possible. A prejudice is not a distorting form of thought that must be shaken off before we see the world aright. For Gadamer prejudices are present in all understanding. Against Enlightenment claims that reason, detached from historical and cultural perspective, gives a test for truth, Gadamer claims that we are irredeemably embedded in language and culture – and that the escape to unclouded certainty via rational method is a chimera.

How does Gadamer substantiate the assertion that forms of understanding are always prejudicial and that we cannot make strictly objective claims about the world? Here is where we find his singular contribution to contemporary thought. Understanding is invariably 'hermeneutical', he claims. The term derives from *hermeneutics*, 'the branch of knowledge dealing with interpretation' (Oxford English Dictionary). Historically, hermeneutics was the art of correctly reading and interpreting ancient texts, notably the Bible. In Gadamer's hands hermeneutics becomes a more general procedure for understanding itself, which he terms *philosophical hermeneutics* and characterizes in terms of a 'hermeneutical circle'. The idea of the circle refers to the constantly turning movement between one part of a text and its total meaning. In making sense of a fragment of the text one is always simultaneously interpreting the whole. Gadamer justifies extending the role of hermeneutics, making it a necessary characteristic of any attempt to understand the world, by referring back to the history of hermeneutics and early attempts to codify interpretative practice. Hermeneutics is also a submerged strand running through the history of philosophy. Aristotle's account of *phronesis* or 'practical wisdom' is a case in point. In becoming moral we are habituated into a moral tradition, Aristotle asserts, but the moral agent is always confronted with situations that go beyond the regularities of habit. This oscillation between habit and novelty is similar to the dynamic of the hermeneutical circle.

Gadamer's principal authority for his claims is his teacher Martin Heidegger. In *Being and Time* Heidegger shows how interpretation of the world is impossible without pre-understanding. Against Descartes he shows that understanding is not worked out in the privacy of consciousness but through our being in the world. But if all understanding is interpretation, it is still guided by what Gadamer calls a 'fusion of horizons'. A text, or any thing or event within the world we interpret, has its own *horizon* of meaning. Interpretation is sited within the mutual horizon of the interpreter and the thing to be interpreted.

The modernist thought that understanding depends on a detachment from tradition effected by rational method is undermined when viewed from the hermeneutical perspective. For

Gadamer, truth is not method but simply what happens in dialogue. Acts of interpretation are dialogical, a ceaseless conversation that is, within tradition. The interpreter projects provisional
meanings but these are disturbed and re-defined when the interpreter's own prejudices are questioned by the horizon of the text
or the partner in dialogue. Ultimately, Gadamer claims, meanings can never be complete. Another consequence of Gadamer's
'fusion of horizons' is a re-defined relationship to the past. If all
understanding is dialogue, it is as much a conversation with the
past as with the future. So, the past is not 'a foreign country' but
a continuous effect in the present as contemporary language and
that of antiquity work together within a common tradition. Here
again the idea of methodological detachment is, for Gadamer, a
non-starter. We cannot find an Archimedean point outside
culture and language in our pursuit of truth, as our prejudices,
the conditions of understanding, are part of what we seek to
make comprehensible.

Gadamer's questioning of rational method rejects the view that
reason stands behind language. Cultural products (including art)
and the natural world are not objects for rational investigation
but voices within the fabric of an interminable conversation.[1]

I hope this thumbnail sketch gives a useful overview. Sometimes a
quick snapshot of this kind is a useful place to start if one has never
seriously studied the work of a thinker before. What stands out in
this all too brief description of Gadamer's achievements is unease
about the modern world's inherited conceptions of truth and reason,
a revival and revision of ancient hermeneutics, and a nostalgic back-
wards glance at a vanished pre-modern world. A philosophical position so evidently setting its face against the modern world must seem
doomed from the start. In actual fact, in an odd way, Gadamer's
questioning the foundations of philosophical modernism puts him,
strangely, in the same position of those sceptical thinkers of the last
20 years or so called 'postmodern'. This is a theme I will explore in
greater detail in later chapters.

In seeking to position a thinker within the co-ordinates of current
debate and introduce his work to a new audience it is instructive to
speculate upon his place in the history of modern philosophy. Of
course such assessments are always difficult to make without the *grav-
itas* of history bearing down upon the possibly ephemeral. It is always

possible that a thinker is only able to speak to his/her contemporaries and is ultimately found to have no voice for generations other than the present one. The Chinese remark about it being too early to reflect upon the influence of the French Revolution springs to mind here. I suspect Gadamer's work will endure when that of many of his contemporaries has become no more than a footnote in the history of the philosophy of the twentieth century. In some ways his work, like Nietzsche's 'thoughts out of season', will take some time before the full force of his writings are appreciated – especially by those working in the Anglophone philosophical traditions. As matters stand at the moment, Gadamer's work receives limited recognition in the English-speaking world and the full impact of his achievement has yet to be felt. In the next section of this chapter I want to point to some of the reasons why Gadamer has yet to make his mark.

GADAMER AND ANALYTIC PHILOSOPHY

Gadamer passed away in 2002 after a prodigiously long life. Although hailed as the Grand Old Man of philosophy and letters in his native Germany, when he died he had achieved something of a following in Europe and North America but was known only to a limited circle of Anglophone philosophers, social theorists and literary critics. As a world-renowned philosopher his is not a name to conjure with: he is hardly on a par with the likes of the acknowledged giants of twentieth-century thought, such as Wittgenstein or Heidegger. There are many historical and cultural reasons to account for this lack of fame outside the German-speaking world. First and foremost Gadamer does not fit the bill for a stereotypical Anglo-Saxon philosopher. Despite spending a lifetime studying and teaching mainly ancient philosophy, notably interpretations of the Greek classics of Plato and Aristotle, Gadamer's conception of philosophy was exceptionally broad, reaching well beyond the conventional range of logic and epistemology, the staple fare of his English and American counterparts. Gadamer was essentially a philosopher of culture or at least a philosopher for whom the basis of culture and its achievements was a matter for reflection and enquiry. He addresses questions about the basis of the human sciences themselves and how they stand in relation to the natural sciences. His range of vision goes well beyond the technicalities of much modern philosophy that for all its complexity frequently stays myopically within the ambit of a limited, specialist, field of operation zealously guarding its own little academic patch and fighting off scientific and other potential usurpers.

In the present age scientific rationality is all-pervasive. Despite challenges from theology and opposing cultural forces such as environmentalism, alternative and new age philosophies the scientific worldview still holds sway, and assumes itself to be the language of authority and legitimacy in the modern age: the language by which all other voices are to be tested and, ultimately, found wanting. What is considered thinkable and acceptable in any age has to pass the test of reason, which is often the postivistically inclined question about testability and verification. For many the scientific worldview is self-evidently true and carries its own authority. On the other hand there is a whole tradition of thought which has sought to question such self-evidence by placing the whole scientific, and some would say Enlightenment, project into question.

Since the eighteenth century, with the ascendancy of scientific thought, what we might term literary culture, the authority of classical and canonical texts, art and literature, has taken on a subordinate position. Once the expression of, in the case of the Bible, the word of God, and to a lesser extent with literature, the supreme achievements of humanity (what Matthew Arnold in *Culture and Anarchy*, describing the cultural achievements of every age, called 'the best that is thought and written'), were, after the scientific revolution, placed in question as peerless authorities of wisdom and truth.

The great expression of this new authority is to be found in René Descartes's *Discourse on Method* where he speaks, in the revolutionary new language of scientific modernity, of his autobiographical distrust of literature and the classics. The world of letters he assumes is based not on self-evident reasoning but the vagaries of nothing more certain than ancient speculation and questionable opinion. Against this Descartes depicts man as a thinking machine capable of arriving at the kind of certainty to be found in geometry. This dream of Descartes', to model the truth of man on the procedures of logic and geometry, largely came to fruition over the ensuing centuries and provided the guiding thread for knowledge over the next 300 years.

Scientific rationalism, and its practical consequences technology, may still dominate in the modern world but the theoretical and philosophical justification it depended upon in the ideas of Descartes has come in for profound criticism. This is particularly true of both modern continental and analytic philosophy where Descartes, in accounts of the rise of philosophical modernism, is invariably the villain of the piece. There was no one identifiable point at which this subversion of the Cartesian orthodoxy commenced but we can see it being formulated in the system of Hegel and the seminal satirization of the claims of reason by Nietzsche in the nineteenth century. Following this, almost every significant thinker within the twentieth century starts out with an attack upon Cartesian foundationalism[2] and then proceeds to elaborate a system of truth, which unpicks the foundations of knowledge in self-authenticating reason. What many contemporary thinkers, in the continental tradition, succeed in doing, wittingly or unwittingly, is to re-assert the importance of a bookish, literary culture via a challenge to science and a vindication of the importance and truthfulness of art, and literature as embodying forms of knowledge and truth at variance to a simplistic picture of science as the accurate picture of everything. The English author C.P. Snow famously dubbed the split the 'two cultures' and he showed how literary culture plays second fiddle to its opposite number in the sciences. The split Snow adverted to was a gap in culture discussed well before the mass society of the 1950s. Whereas for Snow the split was cultural it is possible to show how this division has its roots in philosophical theory going back to romanticism, a forerunner to the various latter-day rejections of enlightenment thought.

This division between a scientific and a literary culture provides a crucial backdrop to an exposition of the work of Gadamer in particular but more generally it gives access to the origins of that tired old division between 'continental' and 'analytic' philosophy which in itself explains why Gadamer's work has not received the attention it deserves. Why is this so? Let us begin by looking first at the relationship between scientific and literary cultures and the division within philosophy between so-called continental and analytic movements or traditions. This will take us on to a consideration of one of the importances of Gadamer's work: how one can use his version of hermeneutics to build bridges across the seemingly cavernous and unbridgeable divide between the literary and the scientific cultures. For Gadamer, ultimately there is only one culture or mainstream tradition and it should always be possible for its disparate parts to find a common idiom and reach an understanding, however limited and provisional that understanding might be. Going even further than the two cultures, hermeneutics affirms the possibility of dialogue between hostile and seemingly irreconcilable national cultures;

trans-cultural understanding and dialogue is always aimed at, if never perfectly achieved. Gadamer reminds us that despite endless recent discussion of alterity and difference, in the wake of deconstruction, we can still look to the things we share in common and which unites us as a species without making concessions to the abstract notion of a common humanity.

At the risk of gross oversimplification we can speak of analytic philosophy's subservience to the model of science. The style of philosophy we now know as analytic, which sees its task as the examination of language as a means to truth, starts out from a view of language that assumes the possibility of an accurate replication of the world via the linguistic means we have at our disposal to talk about that world. This assumption of exact replication is parallel to scientific method's assumption of certainty in its procedural methods. This was the dream of Wittgenstein in his pioneering classic of early philosophical analysis, the *Tractatus Logico-Philosophicus*. A consequence of this view of language is that literary, metaphorical and rhetorical techniques and devices are seen to be nothing more than obstacles and distortions that only a logically perfect language can expose and eradicate.

Continental philosophy has always been wary of empirical approaches to knowledge and generally distrusts the model of knowledge where the passive monadic subject builds up, over time and experience, with care and attention to possible distortions, an accurate picture of the world. More often than not in continental thought, language is fundamentally expressive, expressing and constituting the human social world long before it is able to describe and represent it – and even that description and representation is not neutral but coloured by the culturally conditioned manner of expression. For this reason mainstream European philosophy has always been more receptive to accommodating artistic and literary expressions of the real and the true; in fact one is tempted to say that receptivity to the literary and the artistic are more evidently defining characteristics of 'continental thought' than considerations of national boundaries and geographical location.[3] The dream of a logically perfect language has always been of limited attraction to those with a more expansive and soul-searching picture of language and its creative and imaginative possibilities. Art, poetry, literature and metaphor are not mere embellishments to language – as characterized by a teasing and ironic Plato in the final book of the *Republic* – but the lifeblood of language itself. Philosophers working in the analytic tradition tend to read Plato straight and look upon literary works as language in its fallen state. Gadamer has always excluded himself from the analytic way of doing philosophy and for this reason his work in general, but his work on language in particular, has not received adequate treatment in the English-speaking world.[4] Gadamer's philosophical position, emerging as it does from the continental traditions of hermeneutics and phenomenology, has few obvious points of contact with much that passes for philosophy within the analytic tradition. What may alarm many analytic philosophers is Gadamer's unapologetic allegiance to the work of Martin Heidegger. For many analytic thinkers, following in the footsteps of Rudolf Carnap, Heidegger is a philosopher to be treated with a large degree of caution as he represents European philosophy at its most opaque and obscure.[5]

To be sure the range of ideas and questions are actually much the same in both philosophical traditions but the approaches, idioms and styles seem worlds apart as Heidegger's writings often demonstrate. But they are not necessarily so. A central claim made in this introduction to Gadamer's work is that he is vitally important as a bridge-builder between the two – often warring and mutually suspicious – traditions. This may seem an extraordinary assertion to make as there is a clear and evident unease from the opposite direction in Gadamer's work around the central tenets of analytic philosophy, but I will seek to justify the position I advance in later chapters. One immediate reason for Gadamer's failure to make his mark in the Anglophone philosophical world is his distance from the prevailing style of analysis, which models itself on the procedures and methods of natural science. There might even be doubts from certain quarters, as there clearly is around Heidegger's work, that what Gadamer does is philosophy. So what does he do? He works in the tradition of hermeneutics and emerging from that his work is know as philosophical hermeneutics.[6]

Philosophical hermeneutics is a phrase with little currency in the English-speaking world and this is another reason for excluding Gadamer from the philosophical canon. Philosophical hermeneutics grows out of a much earlier activity, known simply as hermeneutics. This is defined by the Concise Oxford Dictionary as 'the branch of knowledge that deals with interpretation, esp. of Scripture or literary texts'. So hermeneutics starts out life as a procedure or technique for interpreting sacred and classical texts. Interpretation involves more than the philological investigation into the historical origins and meanings of words, it can be seen to be an element in the process, act or event of understanding itself. This is one of Gadamer's key contributions to contemporary thought. His commitment to the idea that all understanding is interpretation demonstrates that hermeneutics is involved in all acts of understanding, that is, hermeneutics goes well beyond the reaches of textual interpretation. In fact for Gadamer hermeneutics is universal: what happens when we interpret a text is what happens when we seek to understand anything in our cultural social world be it the meaning of life or the more mundane interpretation of everyday objects, ideas and situations. Reading is interpretation, looking is interpretation, thinking is interpretation; interpretation is not a special activity confined to the unravelling of difficult texts it is an aspect of all forms of human understanding. To go back to the distinction I offered earlier between a scientific and a literary culture. Gadamer is more concerned with 'understanding' than the more limited and possibly technical 'knowledge'. Maybe this gives the key to Gadamer's view of philosophy. Certain versions of philosophy may see their task as the enquiry into the nature and limits of human knowledge, as it undoubtedly was in the period of high modernism in the eighteenth century. But understanding, the process and acts of understanding, which occur daily in our attempts to make sense of our world, is ceaselessly at work for hermeneutics. Gadamer sees in the everyday appropriation and negotiation of the world hermeneutical understanding at work. For this reason practical activity and philosophy are not too far apart and again for this reason Gadamer's work is quite far removed from the technicalities of analytic philosophy. And again because hermeneutical understanding and interpretation are evident in all practical activity and concerns, the distinction between the literary and the scientific breaks down. Understanding is larger than either the literary or the scientific because both are forms of human understanding. Gadamer has been accused of being anti-scientific and hostile to science. This is not a fair criticism. What he does do is to question the authority of science and scientific discourse as the only legitimate voice in the conversation of human understanding. He is also dismissive of 'scientism'. In making philosophy more hermeneutical Gadamer seeks to bring out the interpretive dimension to all activities – academic and otherwise. Those quick to synthesize and use hermeneutics have been the practitioners of the social sciences and literary theory where Gadamer's work, since the early 1970s, made its mark. Philosophy has been rather slower to pick up on the importance of Gadamer's work. In the social sciences hermeneutics was used as a bulwark against the excesses of positivistic sociology: Jürgen Habermas's debate with Gadamer was a debate essentially amongst kindred spirits despite Habermas's Marxian critique of Gadamer's apparent conservativism. The importance of philosophical hermeneutics for literary theory stems from Gadamer's unfashionable return to the view of art as truth, his respect for the construction of canons, and his celebration of the lyric poem as a more instructive encounter with language than the arid propositional assertions of a certain kind of philosophy.

One final point on the failure of Gadamer to achieve full recognition in the eyes of Anglophone philosophy has to do with his historicism. Gadamer, following in a line of thought from Vico and Hegel in the eighteenth and nineteenth centuries to Foucault and Oakeshott in the more recent period, stresses the importance of the past as an irreducible moment in human thought: all understanding is in some sense historical. In the English-speaking world this stance in generally questioned on the grounds that a certain kind of historicism has been discredited; however, the more fertile and interesting versions have generally been ignored.[7] Once again we need to go back to the idea of science as a dominant paradigm for analytically inclined philosophers. Scientific method gives rise to a misplaced optimism – triumphalism even – about the possibilities of progress and advancement of human thought and its application to technology and science. Put simply, it is wholly forward looking and regards the past as a dark region of ignorance, a quaint epoch of the infancy of the human spirit of antiquarian value for studying the origins of thought but of no direct value to contemporary thought. What Gadamer seeks to reclaim is the inevitable connection the present and future have with the past. The past is not a 'foreign country', as L.P. Hartley once described it: it is very much the home ground on which all our thoughts and actions are played out. Gadamer's hermeneutics depends upon the idea of a constantly re-worked dialogue between past and present and this position cannot be reconciled to the scientific outlook, which takes for granted a world unmediated and undistorted by the shifting sands of historical truth. On the other hand, for Gadamer truth is historical and the timeless world of scientific belief is no more than a chimera. For those critical of Gadamer he is guilty of abolishing truth or at least so relativizes it that the word truth no longer has comprehensible meaning. Bearing these points in mind, we can see how the idiom and style of Gadamer's thought (though I will claim later not the substance) is unfamiliar to a good deal of English language philosophy. I shall claim, admittedly controversially, that a philosophical approach guided by the paradigm of science is invariably, like certain visions of science itself, univocal, confidant, combative even. Gadamer's historicist position, stressing our deep attachment to tradition, has a style of thought which is fallibilist, open-ended, conversational, and, most importantly, attached to the view that the future is obscure and human thought is fragile and constantly overawed and outmanoeuvred by the contingency of things.

THE STRUCTURE OF THE CHAPTERS

In the following chapters I will seek to justify many of the positions I have already outlined by placing Gadamer's ideas in a historical context and by an exposition of his ideas as they are worked out in his major writings. To this end Chapter 1 begins with a biography outlining the milestones in Gadamer's very long – but in some ways rather uneventful – life as a typical German university professor.

Biography is often a useful inroad into the thought of a philosopher whatever may be said to the contrary.[8] Basic facts about a life enable one to place the person within a specific cultural and historical context. It is important to appreciate the milieu in which Gadamer worked. Not only did his working life span two centuries but also he worked during some of the most world-changing events of the modern age. Gadamer lived through the cataclysm of the Third Reich. His decision not to leave Germany during this period has been given a good deal of attention recently. The alleged reasons for not emigrating have been accepted in the past but a new generation of scholars have taken him to task on this matter claiming that his hermeneutical work gives intellectual respectability to Nazism. This chapter proceeds to assess this position but finds the recent Orozco–Wolin critique of Gadamer in relation to Nazism groundless and somewhat fanciful. This chapter also offers a brief intellectual biography tracing some of Gadamer's influences: his early schooling in neo-Kantianism, his introduction to phenomenology and most influential of all falling under the spell of the revolutionary 'existential' ideas of his teacher and later friend, Martin Heidegger.

Chapter 2 examines the role of method in modern philosophy. Starting in the seventeenth century philosophy embarked on a search for a sure and certain method for proceeding in its task of discovering truth. The quest for an unassailable method, and its influence on the development of modern philosophy, provides important background to Gadamer. His magnum opus, *Truth and Method*, examines method and offers a radical critique. This critique takes its inspiration from many sources, not the least of which is Heidegger's radical reworking of the histories of modern philosophy. Of the many aspects of Heidegger's re-thinking the history of modern philosophy is his turn to hermeneutics.

Chapter 3 is entitled 'From hermeneutics to philosophical hermeneutics'. As a preamble to Gadamer's 'philosophical' hermeneutics, we confront the question, 'What is hermeneutics?' The chapter follows the history of hermeneutics from its modern origins in the hermeneutical and theological writings of Friedrich Schleiermacher to the works of Wilhelm Dilthey where it takes a distinctly historicist turn. The chapter ends with an examination of the critical position Gadamer adopts in relation to his predecessors; notably he takes them to task for their failure to disengage from subjectivist interpretation in the case of Schleiermacher and the quest for scientific respectability in the case of Dilthey. He sees in early hermeneutics the heavy hand of methodological and procedural exactitude and seeks to develop an account of interpretive practice free from all dependence upon such limiting and distorting procedures. The biggest single influence upon Gadamer is Martin Heidegger. Heidegger is responsible for the crucial phenomenological and existential turn in hermeneutical thought, which Gadamer utilizes in the elaboration of his own philosophical hermeneutics. It is from Heidegger's reading of the 'hermeneutical circle' that Gadamer is able to expose the shortcomings of any philosophical practice dependent upon a quasi-scientific method.

In Chapter 4 the focus is upon the principal work which established Gadamer's reputation as a key thinker in the twentieth century, namely, *Truth and Method*. In this work Gadamer illustrates, through a detailed engagement with the history of modern philosophy, how traditional hermeneutics, as it were, took a wrong turn. By implicating itself with the search for a scientifically respectable methodology it misconceives the nature of interpretation and understanding. What Gadamer elaborates upon is the nature of that misconception and how the move to a philosophical hermeneutics is only possible via Heidegger's existential and phenomenological account of the famous 'hermeneutical circle'. *Truth and Method* is a very detailed (and often meandering!) work full of profound insight and novel readings of figures and ideas in the history of philosophy giving rise to questions about the meaning of the history of philosophy itself. As well as offering an overview of the central themes and ideas in this masterwork, the chapter examines why this single book represents a new departure in hermeneutics and philosophy. If one were asked what *Truth and Method* is about a short answer would be hard to find. The title is probably the immediate key to unravelling this puzzle. Some commentators have suggested that *Truth or Method* might easily have been the work's title; certainly a central tension or opposition between truth and method is at play in the work and the two do not sit easily together in Gadamer's work.

Since the birth of the modern period, roughly in the middle of the seventeenth century, philosophical and scientific activity has depended upon the elaboration of a correct method or procedure. Descartes can be seen to be doing for philosophy what Newton did for natural science, that is, to give it rules for the direction of thought. The importance of the establishment of a correct method in philosophy has, despite incursions from the various unorthodox quarters, held sway for the last 300 years. What *Truth and Method* succeeds in doing is to question the authority of method by showing how truth, far from being revealed by method, is in fact overshadowed and obscured by it. Gadamer focuses on three modes of experience; art, historical understanding and language are the three principal routes by which truth is disclosed. Here truth is far from the erroneous forms dreamt up by scientific rationality and the orthodox thinking of modernity. The dethroning of a traditional conception of truth is a key part of Gadamer's achievement. And the consequences this has for the way we understand art, historicity and language are far-reaching and profound. To many philosophers the dethroning of truth is heretical as it opens the floodgates to unacceptable forms of relativism, that is, the philosophical view that there are no absolute truths as all belief systems or cultures are relative to each other. If Gadamer is saying all truth is interpretation and all interpretation is historical then truth is consequently relativized and when truth is relativized it is tantamount to saying there is no truth!

Also in Chapter 4, 'Truth without method', more detail of the argumentation of *Truth and Method* is given. The focus here is upon the importance of history and tradition to understanding. The key notions of the 'fusion of horizons' and 'effective historical consciousness' are examined and explained in some detail. Central here is Gadamer's explanation of the possibility of understanding the past from the site of the present, and his stress upon understanding as conversation and dialogue with aspects, past and present, of tradition.

In Chapter 5, 'Gadamer on language and linguisticality', the focus is upon the final section of *Truth and Method* entitled 'The ontological shift of hermeneutics guided by language'. Although one third of the book is explicitly concerned with language, Gadamer's 'philosophy of language', a term he would hate for good reasons, is seldom discussed. This chapter thematizes language as an important aspect of Gadamer's work and takes seriously his dictum 'Being that can be understood is language'.

Chapter 6, 'Gadamer's aesthetics', turns to his treatment of art in *Truth and Method* where it is characterized as one of the experiences of truth that subverts the search for methodized truth. In later developments Gadamer speaks of art as 'play', 'festival' and 'symbol': these ideas are discussed briefly. The chapter concludes by concentrating upon the special role Gadamer reserves for the poetic word, specifically the language of lyric poetry.

Chapter 7, 'The later Gadamer', examines Gadamer's work post-1960, that is, after the publication of *Truth and Method*. As with many thinkers there is an early and a late period. In Gadamer's case he does not repudiate his earlier work, but it would be more accurate to say that he refines it and advances beyond it. We might see *Truth and Method* as the (late) flowering of earlier Gadamer – after all he was 60 when the work was published – and his many essays thereafter as 'late' Gadamer. What characterizes late Gadamer is a willingness to 'regionalize' a hitherto generalized hermeneutics. Some critics have spoken of a move in the later work to a more 'practical' hermeneutics. In the Foreword to the Second Edition of *Truth and Method* Gadamer notes that his hermeneutics gives little in the way of practical guidance and application. His 'real concern was and is philosophical: not what we do or what we ought to do, but what happens to us over and above our wanting and doing.' (*TM*, p. xxviii). He does not change substantially from this position but his work after *Truth and Method* focuses in distinct areas of interpretive practice and some critics have characterized the later work as 'applied hermeneutics'.[9] The application of hermeneutics is first and foremost to the interpretation of poetry and the aesthetic.[10] There are also studies of education[11] and medical practice.[12] For Gadamer, the university represents a paradigm of civilized dialogue and conversation, which is at the heart of hermeneutics. In his work on health and medicine he seeks to retrieve a rapidly dwindling sense of the medical practitioner as hermeneuticist as medicine itself falls victim to the entrapments of scientific method. When all is said and done Gadamer wants to show that all understanding is more of a practical art, and all that that entails, than it is a science, the status of which is ultimately no more certain and fixed than the alternatives. The themes of 'solidarity' and 'hope' occupied him in later life; the chapter concludes with some reflection on the importance of these for Gadamer.

The final chapter, 'Fellow travellers and critics', concludes with an examination of some of the criticisms to which Gadamer's position has been subjected. As well as the charges of relativism there is a cluster of criticisms from various quarters. E.D. Hirsch, the literary critic, accuses Gadamer of abolishing objectivity and meaning by making language itself relative. Further, for Hirsch, Gadamer conflates meaning and significance. The significance of a text, Hirsch asserts, changes, but its meaning does not. Gadamer's hermeneutics allows for the possibility, nay necessity, of a text's meaning changing over time.

Gadamer's work has been subjected to criticisms from the political and theoretical left. *Truth and Method* makes much of the notion of tradition. What obsession with method neglects is the simple fact that much understanding of the world is transmitted via tradition rather than a context-less, a-historical method. But to dissolve all thought into the overarching 'tradition' is to deny the possibility of critique, that central feature of the modernity: Gadamer is portrayed here as a counter-Enlightenment thinker. Finally, Jacques Derrida has criticized Gadamer by seeing in his hermeneutics too much charity, trust and goodwill. Hermeneutical understanding depends upon a measure of flexibility, interpretive 'wiggle-room' if you will. Derrida, taking his leads from Nietzsche, counters this with what Paul Ricoeur aptly termed the 'hermeneutics of suspicion'; there is no place in Gadamer's work for a hermeneutics of suspicion. This ties in with Jürgen Habermas's putative move beyond hermeneutics to a more distrustful – suspicious even – ideology-critique.

By way of a conclusion I look at the future prospects for the work of Gadamer and hermeneutics generally. I suggest that the wide gap between analytic and continental philosophy can be bridged through Gadamer.[13]

NOTES

1 See Baggini and Stangroom (2004), pp. 100–2.
2 Heidegger and, in the analytic tradition, Ryle and Wittgenstein in the twentieth century produce the most influential attacks upon Descartes.
3 The label continental is often misleading. For example, one of the best representatives of early continental thought was the English poet Coleridge!
4 Exceptions include Lawn (2004).
5 Carnap (1978) famously accused Heidegger of formulating metaphysical pseudostatements such as 'The Nothing itself Nothings'.
6 The subtitle of Gadamer's key work *Truth and Method* is 'Elements of a philosophical hermeneutics', curiously missing from the English translations.
7 Karl Popper's critique in *The Poverty of Historicism* pertains to those strictly deterministic social theories which claim to make predictive pronouncements about the future of society based on of the application of strict causal laws. This kind of historicism deserves to be exposed but the more general variety where understanding is taken to be deeply historical and the present owes much of its character to the past is less easily undermined. On the various versions of historicism see Jonathan Rée's essay 'The vanity of historicism' (1991).
8 Heidegger speaking about the history of philosophy once made the following extraordinary assertion: 'The personality of a philosopher is of interest only to this extent: he was born at such and such a time, he worked, and died' (quoted in Grondin (2003b)).
9 The subtitle of Misgeld and Nicholson (1992) is 'Applied Hermeneutics'.
10 Gadamer (1986b).
11 Various essays in Misgeld and Nicholson (1992) in the section entitled 'The philosopher in the university'.
12 Gadamer (1996).
13 This is the kind of position I advocate in *Wittgenstein and Gadamer: Towards a Post-Analytic Philosophy of Language* (2004).

CHAPTER 1

WHO IS GADAMER?[1]

Hans-Georg Gadamer died peacefully at the University Hospital in Heidelberg, Germany, on 13 March 2002. Born in 1900, he was 102 years old; had he been born one year earlier his life would have spanned three centuries. As an active academic, university professor, classicist and originator of 'philosophical hermeneutics', his work was exceptionally well regarded in his own country and in later years he was regarded as the Grand Old Man of German philosophy. Shortly after his death Gadamer's family received a 'telegram of condolence'[2] from Pope John Paul II, this despite notional attachment to protestant Lutheranism. Also tributes of praise were sent from some of the most influential philosophers and intellectuals in the continental tradition. Significantly, apart from respectful obituaries[3] in the British and American quality newspapers, his death passed virtually unnoticed in the English-speaking world. Even now there has yet to be a single conference in the UK or the USA celebrating the life and work of this remarkable man and, as yet, nothing befitting the stature of the man has been planned. As Gadamer, the man, is still a mystery this chapter will concentrate on the details of his life and works.

HANS-GEORG GADAMER: A LONG LIFE IN BRIEF

Hans-Georg Gadamer was born in Marburg in Germany on 11 February 1900 into a middle-class family. His father Johannes Gadamer was at that time a struggling scientist working in Marburg University. Two years later the family moved east to Breslau, now Wrocław in Poland, where Johannes was elevated to the post of professor. Gadamer's early life was surrounded by domestic tragedy as first his only sibling, his sister Ilse, died in infancy, and then his mother died from diabetes two years later when Gadamer was four. A year later his father re-married and by all accounts, including his own, he was unable to feel close to his stepmother Hedwig (*née* Heillich). Gadamer's education at the Holy Ghost School in Breslau was typical for a person of his class and background and his formal education at the Holy Ghost Gymnasium was completed shortly before the end of the First World War in 1918. The same year he matriculated at the University of Breslau and studied, much to the disappointment of his scientific-minded father, a broad introduction to the humanities. This included history, philosophy, literature (mainly German), music, languages and art history. Gadamer's love of the arts and his later decision to work in the humanities was, apparently, a constant source of worry, and no doubt irritation, to Gadamer's rather philistine father. In fact when Johannes was on his deathbed and Gadamer was a philosophy student under Heidegger's tutelage, the teacher was summoned to give a verdict on whether the young Gadamer would make a career of philosophy. Apparently Heidegger spoke well of his promising student at this time, although his opinion was to change at a later stage as we will see.

The general education in the humanities Gadamer received played a key part in his intellectual development for his later influential philosophical work in hermeneutics was, in some sense, an attempt to vindicate and hold onto that ancient idea of education as an initiation into the cultural reference points of Western civilization rather than the more modernist notion of education as accumulated specialist knowledge of the sciences. Evidently, from an early age the young Gadamer had a passion for literature and the arts generally. Was this a conscious or unconscious reaction to his father's strong commitment to natural science and indifference to the wider culture?

Isaiah Berlin's notion that all seminal thinkers essentially effect parricide by seeking to kill the ideas of a symbolic or actual father may be a helpful thought here when seeking to make sense of Gadamer's love of the humanities and snubbing of the sciences. Many critics have accused Gadamer's philosophy of being anti-science. This is an oversimplistic judgement but there is an evident suspicion towards a culture dominated by scientific rationality.

In 1919 Johannes Gadamer received a chair at the University of Marburg and Hans-Georg began studies in philosophy with the neo-Kantian scholar Paul Natorp, in the same university. He wrote his dissertation on 'The nature of pleasure according to Plato's dialogues' under Natorp. In 1922 Gadamer was afflicted by polio, which swept through Marburg (and well beyond) at this time. He was kept in isolation for many months and used his time profitably reading philosophy: amongst other things he worked through Edmund Husserl's phenomenological classic the *Logical Investigations* (Gadamer was to meet Husserl the following year). The effect of polio was to leave its mark on Gadamer for the rest of his life as he was to walk with a pronounced limp from this time on.

GADAMER AND HEIDEGGER

In 1922 the most important event in Gadamer's intellectual development took place: he met Martin Heidegger in Freiburg. Heidegger was to have a pronounced effect on Gadamer's thinking from this time on and Heidegger's influence on his future development is profound and far-reaching. Heidegger's reputation at this time, as a charismatic teacher and new voice in philosophy, was gaining rapidly, and in the following year Gadamer moved to Freiburg to attend Heidegger's classes. They struck up a tentative friendship, albeit, initially, of the master–pupil variety and Gadamer served as his mentor's assistant first in Freiburg and later in Marburg in the early 1920s when Heidegger took up a new position there. Spellbound by his magnetic teacher the eager scholar sought to make his mark but was soon rebuffed as his teacher failed to be impressed by his performance. Heidegger made this plain in a letter to Gadamer in 1924 where he made a cutting comment as much about Gadamer's character as it was about the unimpressive quality of his philosophical work. 'If you cannot summon sufficient toughness toward yourself', wrote Heidegger, commenting on Gadamer's academic performance, 'nothing will come of you.'[4] Utterly crushed by this personal slight he began to doubt his own ability to do important philosophical work and reverted to more philologically oriented studies. Gadamer took a very long time to recover from this snub and remained philosophically inert for many years due to feelings of self-doubt. 'For a long time, writing tormented me', came a confession in later life, 'I always had the damned feeling that Heidegger was looking over my shoulder.'[5] In fact he claimed to have abandoned philosophy at this time in order to re-establish his connections with philology and classical thought and languages, a move away, that is, from the clutches of a harshly critical

Martin Heidegger. Despite the rift, Heidegger agreed to supervise Gadamer's *Habilitation* thesis submitted in 1929 under the title 'Interpretation of Plato's *Philebus*'. This was Gadamer's first substantial piece of philosophical work, published in 1931 under the title *Plato's Dialectical Ethics*. During the war years Gadamer had little contact with Heidegger although after 1945 they re-established contact which lasted until Heidegger's death in 1976. Heidegger remained the most important figure in Gadamer's intellectual development and no other influence had quite the same impact upon his mature philosophical work.

GADAMER AND THE NAZIS

Both Gadamer and Heidegger remained in Germany during the Third Reich but whereas Heidegger's shameful tangle with National Socialism is well documented Gadamer's relationship to the Nazis is much more sketchy and vague. Heidegger joined the Nazi Party in 1933 and as a consequence readily, albeit to the surprise of many of his students, took up the politically sensitive post of Rector at the University of Freiburg. His thought and writings during this year show evident signs of total acceptance of Nazi ideology. Although Heidegger was to sever links with the Nazi Party shortly after this time, in later life, to his shame, he never apologized for his conduct during this period, nor did he publicly accept that he was guilty, to put it kindly, of a monstrous error of judgement.[6]

Concerning Gadamer's conduct during the Nazi period, his own version was that he worked diligently throughout the war years on a small income. He had married Frida Katz in 1923 and in 1926 his first daughter Jutta was born.[7] Life was hard during this period, as he had to make do with little more than a modest academic income and to compound the misery hardship was widespread; this was the time of a financial crisis throughout Germany. He kept a low profile and accepted incremental academic advancement when it came his way. After the war, having avoided formal connection with the National Socialist Party, 'denazification' was unnecessary. This was not the case with Heidegger who was prevented from teaching for five years after the war. So untainted was Gadamer that the Russians supported his election to the position of Rector of the University of Leipzig (in what was to become East Germany) in the immediate post-war period of reconstruction. Leipzig was under Soviet domination in the initial post-war period and Gadamer moved west as soon as the opportunity arose and when the professorship of Heidelberg, formerly Karl Jasper's position, fell vacant, he took up the post.

Against this generally accepted picture of Gadamer's non-involvement with the Nazis during the war years, recent controversial studies – of questionable academic worth it has to be said – suggest a murkier past. Teresa Orozco[8] and Richard Wolin[9] claim that certain activities during the Third Reich indicate a closer relationship to Nazism than ever admitted publicly by Gadamer. The case against him depends upon the following claims made about his activities during the Nazi period.

He gained professorial positions, it is claimed, by unscrupulously taking over posts of 'furloughed', i.e. sacked, academics of Jewish descent. For example, he accepted the professorship to replace Richard Kroner, the Jewish professor at Kiel. It is asserted that he attended a Nazi summer school for university teachers. He is accused of giving a lecture on Herder (the 'father of German nationalism') in Paris during the occupation. Finally, his 1934 essay 'Plato and the poets' succoured fascist notions of the state and in some way contributed to ideological support for the Nazi regime. Wolin's and Orozco's work represent something of a 'witch hunt' and plausible explanations to counter the various charges are ready to hand. When quizzed about this period Gadamer responded that as a liberal he disliked the regime, stood by his Jewish colleagues and friends, and was left alone by the Nazis for he was not a threat and after all they had no use for philosophers. At the same time Gadamer claims to have followed the familiar path of 'inner emigration' that is, working within the Third Reich but psychologically keeping his distance, emigrating in a metaphorical sense.[10] This last point rings true. Gadamer wrote very little during the period 1933–45 and it is as if he got his head down and made himself invisible; whether he had a duty to combat such indifference to the regime is a moot ethical point. Of the works on Herder and Plato, the Herder essay is not a glorification of the German people and the Plato essay if anything is a warning against the dangers of too powerful a state and thus is, if anything, subversive of Nazism rather than supportive of it. Richard Palmer, a former student of Gadamer's and leading exponent of philosophical hermeneutics in North America, has challenged the claims about his teacher's dubious record during the Nazi period and his intellectual and practical closeness to Nazism in 'A response to Richard Wolin on

Gadamer and the Nazis' (Palmer, 2002). Palmer's view that it is, in the light of the evidence, preposterous to make these claims, is plausible and the facts and hypotheses drawn upon by Wolin to attack Gadamer are largely spurious. In later life Gadamer spoke very little about the Nazi years so to some extent the jury is still out as those attacking Gadamer rely more on conjecture than hard evidence. I suspect it will involve a good deal of further historical work to get a more accurate picture. No doubt with the future publication of Gadamer's complete correspondence and when a good deal more work is done on the contents of university archives during the Nazi period, a fuller picture will emerge.

AFTER THE WAR

Throughout the war years there was little contact with Heidegger but later a personal friendship was re-established lasting from the late 1940s, when Gadamer was Professor of Philosophy in Heidelberg, to the time of Heidegger's death in 1976. Heidegger's rehabilitation from post-war isolation was due, in part, to Gadamer although the popularization of his work by the post-war French thinkers, notably Jean-Paul Sartre and Emmanuel Levinas, was equally important in Heidegger being brought in from the cold. Gadamer organized the 1949 *Festschrift* for Heidegger's sixtieth birthday and was responsible for frequent invitations for Heidegger to lecture in Heidelberg. Unfortunately the master–pupil relationship endured, however, and Gadamer's 'awe' in the presence of his former teacher clearly irked his own students who witnessed his continual subservience to Heidegger.

Although a full professor from a relatively early age he had not published a substantial work since his *Habilitation* thesis and throughout the 1950s he worked diligently but fitfully upon what was to become his *magnum opus*, *Truth and Method*. Gadamer's international reputation started after the publication in 1960 in Germany of *Truth and Method*. From this point onwards he rose from being a little-known commentator on classical Greek philosophy and well-respected university teacher to one of the most important names in what came to be known as 'philosophical hermeneutics'. The work was instantly recognized as an important work in Germany and the debate it sparked off with the emerging young voice in social theory, Jürgen Habermas, added to its widening notoriety.

It was not until 1975 that the work was translated into English and started to make its mark in the American academy, principally amongst literary theorists and social scientists rather than philosophers. By the 1990s the work came to be recognized by many as one of the most important philosophical texts of the twentieth century. It addressed topical but disputed philosophical questions and issues relating to the nature of culture and meaning. It was very much part of the spirit of the age and although it is, in many ways, a backward, almost nostalgic, glance at a world we have lost, it chimed in with the prevalent spirit of postmodernity and this partially explains its notoriety.

RETIREMENT AND INTERNATIONAL ACCLAIM

Gadamer retired from full-time university life in 1968 and at a time when most academics would be thinking of disengaging from professional activities and winding down scholarly commitments Gadamer's international career commenced. *Truth and Method* had put him on the global stage. He became a frequent visitor to the US for many years, notably Boston College, and travelled throughout the world attending conferences and introducing his brand of philosophical hermeneutics to a younger generation of academics. For all the emphasis in Gadamer's work upon tradition and a need to reclaim and retrieve the thoughts and ideas of the pre-modern world Gadamer's work struck a chord with postmodern thinkers. His famous exchange in 1981 with Jacques Derrida in Paris, billed as a confrontation (or was it a showdown?) between hermeneutics and deconstruction, further enhanced Gadamer's reputation as an important thinker despite the fact that the meeting was something of a non-event, and hardly produced the fireworks, no doubt, many were expecting. Even in his later years Gadamer was still active writing papers and attending conferences, giving interviews, the usual trappings of celebrity and notoriety. As well as his more philosophical writings he took a keen interest in literature, especially the interpretation of lyric poetry, and his later reflections on the poets Rilke,[11] Celan,[12] Hölderlin and George[13] bear witness to this enthusiasm.

He died in 2002 at the biblically old age of 102. Even in very old age he remained mentally active and interested in world events. One of his last public statements came in an interview with the German newspaper *Die Welt* when he commented upon the 9/11 events saying, '*Es ist mir recht unheimlich geworden*' ('the world has become quite strange to me').[14] This is one of Gadamer's few expressions of despair as much of his later writing is on hope, not as a theological wish but as necessary secular feature of social life. The strangeness of the world Gadamer speaks of is, perhaps, a momentarily despairing comment upon his principal idea of hermeneutical conversation now rendered potentially obsolete and unworkable in the face of such world-dividing, dialogue-stopping, incomprehensible events. At the heart of philosophical hermeneutics is the promise of something shared, a solidarity behind every disharmony. With 9/11 Gadamer possibly started to doubt this promise.

GADAMER: THE MAN AND HIS WORK

Despite the many works now available on Gadamer it is very difficult to get a full picture of the man: his like and dislikes, his activities outside the academy, his character and personality. He was evidently a quiet and unassuming person yet urbane and gregarious, extremely generous with his time to students and by all accounts a forceful and charismatic teacher. A *bon viveur* he liked good company, good conversation and good wine. He was clearly a cultured man, in the old-fashioned sense of cultured, being knowledgeable about high art, music and literature, especially modern German lyric poetry. Even in the modern world of installations, happenings and conceptual art, Gadamer evidently sought to make sense of these in his writings by showing that no matter how alienating and difficult art works might appear there is always the possibility of dialogue. Art works address us and we have a responsibility to listen.

Gadamer never wrote an autobiography. His *Philosophical Apprenticeships*[15] is more of an intellectual biography, giving thumbnail sketches of his teachers and mentors. Gadamer is always a shadowy presence in this work and the book's motto '*De nobis ipsis silemus*' ('about ourselves we should be silent') – also incidentally used by Francis Bacon, Immanuel Kant and Paul Natorp, one of Gadamer's teachers – says much about Gadamer's modesty and reticence. Even the title *Philosophical Apprenticeships* speaks of Gadamer's diffidence; in good hermeneutical style he sees himself as an eternal apprentice always willing to learn from others and reluctant to impose one's own conception of truth upon the collective truth of a conversation. In hermeneutics the important thing is not to assume a text to be a dumb and silent partner but an active voice in a constant conversation; good hermeneutical practice is to listen to the text and be subordinate to it. In many ways Gadamer's account of his life is one in which he is always the silent witness.

His essay 'Reflections on my philosophical journey', written for the prestigious Library of Living Philosophers,[16] is another quasi-autobiographical piece. Like *Philosophical Apprenticeships* it is a very useful description of the life of Gadamer's mind, his intellectual development and his reflections on his triumphs and weaknesses, but says very little about his likes and dislikes, the music he listened to, the paintings he admired. Again he remains hidden and curiously lifeless. The most illuminating picture of Gadamer, the person, emerges from Jean Grondin's more or less official biography published shortly after Gadamer's death.[17] Easily dismissed as hagiography the Grondin biography gives a sensitive and sympathetic portrait of Gadamer. Written with Gadamer's initially reluctant approval Grondin's work, benefiting from access to most of Gadamer's papers, is the most authoritative so far. And yet it tends to gloss over the war years, accepting without question Gadamer's own account of events.

Other useful brief sketches are Robert Dostal's[18] outline of Gadamer's life and work and Richard Palmer's warm tribute to his teacher in the journal *Symposium*.[19] In many ways his life was pretty uneventful and lacking in the adventure and drama one associates with the likes of Wittgenstein and his constant movement from Cambridge professor to hermit in Norway to architect, schoolteacher and millionaire in Vienna, or Sartre and his tireless political campaigning. Yet Gadamer witnessed some of the greatest upheavals in the modern world and it is astonishing to think he was born in the year Nietzsche died.

Of politics, Gadamer always claimed that he was a good liberal despite attempts to show that his work conservatively defended the political status quo. His liberal credentials are impeccable as the fallibilism at the heart of hermeneutics; the thought that no one view has a monopoly on truth and the advocacy of the free exchange of ideas as paramount in any mature political arrangement strongly echo the father of modern liberalism, John Stuart Mill. I suppose Gadamer's work is conservative in a literal sense of 'keeping', but what is kept, the tradition, is not unchanging and frozen in the past but constantly making its claim upon the present and the future.

In this sense Gadamer is hardly a conservative since novelty and change is at the heart of his hermeneutics. But he doesn't willingly embrace all change. Like Heidegger and Wittgenstein he embraces a politics of cultural critique deriving from Nietzsche which rejects the foundations of industrial society and the rule of technocracy and scientific rationalism.

Concerning religion Gadamer was never hostile to religious belief and faith in his life and work. Although notionally a Protestant he always kept a certain distance from organized religions, and an affirmation of belief, although many would see in his philosophical hermeneutics the resources for such an affirmation. In the interview with *Radical Philosophy* Gadamer is asked: 'It's clear from your writings that you have a tremendous respect for religious experience and religious theory. But it's impossible to tell whether you are a believer. Is that deliberate?' His answer is a straightforward, 'Well, yes it is deliberate.'[20]

As we have already noted *Truth and Method*, Gadamer's key work, was published when he was 60. Prior to this time although his list of published writings was quite short he had worked since the 1930s on the philosophy of Plato and Aristotle. What was revolutionary about his mature work was his ability to use his nascent hermeneutics as a strategy for interpreting ancient texts. His writings on Plato and Aristotle are original and he throws light on Plato by offering a hermeneutical account of the nature of dialogue and why it was Plato used dialogue rather than any other means of communicating his ideas. The standard view that Plato's work defends a universalist account of truth is challenged by Gadamer's stress upon the provisional, tentative and fallible nature of human knowledge and that the dialogue makes this position apparent. As well as this Gadamer undermines the orthodox idea that Aristotle's work, in its mature phase, is a complete repudiation of Platonism. Gadamer succeeds in showing that Aristotle never moves far beyond Plato and the idea of a radical rupture between the two lacks hermeneutical plausibility.[21] As a writer Gadamer's style is elegant and uncluttered. His subject matter may be difficult and his sheer range of erudition and scholarship may impress but his written style is very clear. *Truth and Method* presents the reader with a formidable challenge, if only because the work is so long and desultory, but the arguments are clearly stated and Gadamer's lifelong mission as an educator and pedagogue are evident via his desire to communicate. He seldom lapses into opacity and obscurity even though the structure of *Truth and Method* is at times a little shaky.

Curiously Gadamer wrote very little of substance before his groundbreaking *Truth and Method* in 1960. There are various reasons to account for this. The 'inner emigration' spoken of earlier, the strategy of many academics and intellectuals who did not leave Germany during the Third Reich but maintained a stubborn silence as a kind of passive resistance is partial explanation for Gadamer's failure to produce more than a handful of papers during this period. And after the war Gadamer, in Leipzig, as Rector had a large administrative burden and this kept him away from publishing his research. A more compelling reason for Gadamer's modest output until he had almost reached retirement age was the emphasis he placed upon teaching. In the interview with Jonathan Rée and Christian Gehron for *Radical Philosophy* when asked about whether writing was, for him, a pleasure, he makes the following revealing confession:

> No, it is violence. It is torture. Dialogue is fine. Even an interview! But writing for me is always an enormous self-torture. . . . My main work was published when I was already sixty. My prestige as a teacher was quite high, and I had been a full professor for a long time. But I had not published much work. I invested more of my energy in teaching.[22]

Like Socrates, Gadamer put great emphasis upon philosophy as a practical activity, live conversation, hence his tolerance of interviews and dialogue. In fact philosophy itself, like all interpretive practice, is essentially dialogue, not a systematic treatise or extensive work of theory. In this light we can see why Gadamer found the construction of an extended text so torturous as it would have run against his conception of philosophy as dialogue or conversation. This said, *Truth and Method*, his only extended work, is 500 pages long and pretty heavy going for those without the necessary background in hermeneutical philosophy. Yet despite his difficulties with writing the *Gesammelte Werke*, the complete works in German, runs to a daunting ten volumes. But this is an extensive corpus of essays not tracts and treatises; Gadamer was a writer of occasional pieces, like Montagne, essentially an essayist.

After *Truth and Method* his important English-language collections of essays run as follows. In 1976 two collections appeared:

Hegel's Dialectic: Five Hermeneutical Studies and *Philosophical Hermeneutics*. The year 1980 saw a collection of essays on Plato, dating as far back as the 1930s, entitled *Reason in the Age of Science*. In 1985 the autobiographical *Philosophical Apprenticeships* appeared and in the following year, an important collection of his essays on art and aesthetics, *The Relevance of the Beautiful and Other Essays*. In 1989 a record of Gadamer's relationship to deconstruction and his brief encounter with Jacques Derrida, *Dialogue and Deconstruction*, was published. In 1992 a collection of hermeneutical studies appeared entitled *Hans-Georg Gadamer on Education, Poetry and History*. In 1994 a collection of essays, largely paying homage to his master but at the same time laying out the difference between the two thinkers, was published, entitled *Heidegger's Ways*, and in the same year a series of essays appeared on literary theory and the work of Goethe, Hölderlin, Rilke and Bach, entitled *Literature and Philosophy: Essays in German Literary Theory*. 1996 saw a wistful collection of essays offering a critique, from a hermeneutical perspective, of modern medical practice's turn from dialogical art to inflexible science, entitled *The Enigma of Health: The Art of Healing in a Scientific Age*. It has been suggested that Gadamer himself must have known something of the secrets of this enigma as he was well into his nineties, and in very good health, when this was written. In 1997 interpretations of the difficult lyric poetry of Paul Celan appeared as *Gadamer on Celan*. As well as these essays there were many journal articles and countless interviews, the best of which are collected in *Gadamer in Conversation* and *A Century of Philosophy*.

For an excellent Gadamer bibliography, at least up until 1996, six years before his death, the Library of Living Philosophers compilation is exhaustive and definitive.[23] Another good bibliographical resource, listing books by and about Gadamer, is to be found in Richard Palmer's *Gadamer in Conversation*. An excellent bibliographical resource is Etsuro Makita's *Gadamer Bibliography*, available on the web in German or Japanese, but sadly not yet in English.[24]

NOTES

1 Much of the biographical information for this chapter is taken from the only English-language biography of Gadamer, Jean Grondin's *Hans-Georg Gadamer: A Biography* (2003b).
2 Grondin (2003b), p. 336.

3 See Julian Roberts' obituary in the *Guardian* (18 March 2002) and an unsigned piece in *The Times* (16 March 2002) amongst others.
4 Quoted in Grondin (2003b), p. 117.
5 Quoted in Grondin (2003b), p. 268.
6 For Gadamer's involvement with the Nazis see Wolin (1993) and the work of Victor Farias.
7 This marriage was to fall apart in the 1940s. Gadamer re-married in 1950. His new wife Kate Lekebusch had been his student and assistant. Their daughter Andrea was born in 1956.
8 Orozco (1996).
9 Wolin (2000) and (2003).
10 For the best account of Gadamer's relationship to the Nazis see his interview with Dörte von Westernhagen, 'The real Nazis had no interest in us . . .', in Palmer (2001), pp. 115–32.
11 See 'Mytho-poetic inversion in Rilke's *Duino Elegies*', Connolly and Keutner (1988).
12 See Gadamer (1997).
13 See the various essays on poetry in Part 2, 'Hermeneutics, poetry, and modern culture', in Misgeld and Nicholson (1992).
14 Quoted in Grondin (2003b), p. 335.
15 Gadamer (1985).
16 Hahn (1997).
17 Grondin (2003b).
18 See R. J. Dostal's excellent 'Gadamer: The man and his work', in Dostal (2002).
19 Palmer (2002).
20 Rée (1995), p. 35.
21 The best introductions to Gadamer's readings of Plato and Aristotle are in *Dialogue and Dialectic* (1980) and *The Idea of the Good in Platonic-Aristotelian Philosophy* (1986).
22 Rée (1995), p. 27.
23 Hahn (1996), pp. 556–602.
24 See http://www.ms.kuki.tus.ac.jp/KMSLab/makita/gdmhp/ghp_gabi_d.html.

CHAPTER 2

THE PROBLEM OF METHOD

METHOD AND MODERNITY

The following four chapters aim to explain Gadamer's central ideas in so far as they are expanded in his major work *Truth and Method*. There are countless themes and ideas dealt with in this vast, sprawling book but, as the title indicates, the question of method, and ultimately a questioning of the appropriateness of rigid method, is a central concern to the main argument. This chapter reflects on the notion of method as it rose to prominence in the history of modern philosophy and focuses on the critique of the concept of method Gadamer's hermeneutical approach offers. This will take us to the heart of what is at issue in *Truth and Method*. In order to reclaim overshadowed and repressed accounts of truth from epochs prior to modernity, Gadamer needs to be able to account for the rise of method as a central feature of modern philosophy before he can make a claim about the nature of method itself as the reason why other approaches to truth disappeared without a trace from the cultural landscape. In passing it is worth mentioning that the 'reclamation' and 'retrieval' of repressed or forgotten ideas is of vital importance to Gadamer's *modus operandi*. Philosophical hermeneutics, the position he outlines in *Truth and Method*, advances an important historical thesis. The modern age sees the past only from the perspective of the present and fails to appreciate the extent to which its reading of bygone ages is in danger of obliterating valuable truths. The value of philosophical hermeneutics is not merely to alert us to this danger but to retrieve those ideas – and truths – too readily dispensed with in the name of progress, or advancement, that is, modernity. The modern fixation on method eclipses alternative ways of approaching truth.

DESCARTES AND THE SEARCH FOR METHOD

The year 1637 is often cited as a key date in the history of philosophy. It is the year of the publication of a short tract, one that was to
have such a tremendous impact upon contemporary and subsequent
philosophical thought. The tract *Discours de la Méthode* or *The
Discourse on Method*[1] is so revolutionary because in six short chapters it succeeds in subverting many of the orthodoxies of the earlier
scholastic thought and in bold and unambiguous terms sets the
agenda for a new paradigm of knowledge and truth. A mixture of
Christian thought and Aristotelianism dominated the scholastic philosophy prior to Descartes and his work sought to give philosophical thought the firmer foundations of natural science. What ancient
thought lacked, the seventeenth-century philosophers assumed, was
a methodological procedure with the respectability of the so-called
New Science. It was Descartes who set out to establish it.

Seeking to put human knowledge on the sure and certain footing
of Newtonian natural science, Descartes devised a method for arriving at certainty. He explained in the autobiographical first chapter of
the *Discourse* how he sensed the fabric of knowledge to rest on no
more than 'shaky foundations', in other words, based upon the traditional authorities of ancient Greek philosophy, classical literature
and scriptural, Biblical, authority. In essence Descartes is not actually rejecting ancient authorities – because, he assumes, they rest on
nothing more than unverifiable probabilities, opinions, speculations –
but he is rejecting the legitimacy of textual authority. The importance
of Descartes is his questioning of the legitimacy of texts whose
authority rests on little more than a self-authenticating appeal to the
power of tradition. Descartes inaugurates a seismic move in legitimacy; a paradigm shift from the authority of texts to the authority of
reason. The only true authority he submits to is the authority of
reason and his short work demonstrates how the guiding hand of an
infallible method will ensure truths as certain as those of the natural
sciences and leave behind the unsteady foundations of the literary and
bookish past. The exact terms of his method need not be spelt out
here, although in short they take their cue from the procedures of the
exact sciences of geometry and logic. In essence, Descartes is applying the newly created scientific method not to the external world of
nature but the hitherto unexplored region of philosophical thought.
Establishing both the scope and limits of human thought and the

foundations upon which certain ideas are grounded requires a procedural method on a par with natural science.

The famous 'cogito' argument ('I think therefore I am') is actually arrived at, or more properly derived, using the method Descartes advocates. The 'cogito' argument is the result of the strictly regulated process of doubt its author subjects himself to. In being conscious of all the things he could conceivably doubt he comes to the dramatic conclusion that he cannot actually doubt that he is doubting. This is his conclusion. Doubting is a mode of thinking so the more he doubts the more he actually demonstrates that he is thinking. So whatever Descartes is, whatever his mode of being is, he must, before all else, exist as a thinking thing. From this Descartes assumes it necessarily follows that because he is a thinking thing this must be his essence and that his bodily dimension is merely contingent or secondary: even if he has no body he still remains a thinking thing. Much ink has been spilt arguing over whether the argument for the cogito Descartes advances follows logically or not. What is important from our point of view is this. Descartes's existence as a thinking thing cannot, he argues, be gainsaid. At least one piece of knowledge is absolutely certain, namely, that anything that thinks exists. Let us return to the wisdom of the ancients for a moment. Descartes's problem with the forms of knowledge of the past concerned their dubious claims to legitimacy. How do we know whether the stories of the Bible or the histories of Herodotus are believable or true, we might ask, in the spirit of scientific enquiry? We have no reliable means, from the position of the present, to authenticate the truth credentials of stories conceivably based on little more than hearsay or the fanciful imagination of our forefathers. On the other hand, the veracity of the cogito argument, like the truth of all positions conforming to strict method, are self-authenticating. Descartes says of the cogito argument that he knows it with clarity and distinctness, in other words, it is self-evidently true in the way those ancient texts and writings patently were not. The real problem of ancient wisdom, from the point of view of the new scientific spirit, is that its authority might well rest upon prejudice, superstition, opinion, the vagaries of historical fashion and the ill-informed judgements of those lacking the insights and principles of scientific enquiry. For Descartes, the beauty of his method is that it is apodictic, clearly established and, hence, self-evidently true.

The cogito argument is not just taken to be a vindication of logical truth; it says something about the nature of the self and the forms of knowledge open to it. In turning inwards, by the introspective act Descartes performs upon himself, he proves that true knowledge is an inner attribute of the individual knowing subject. Descartes is important in the history of philosophy not only because he subverted the forms of authority on which the earlier scholasticism depended, and ushered in a defence of human reason as the source of all truth, but also because his new method proved to be so incredibly influential. Without a doubt, the period of intellectual history known as the Enlightenment would not have happened without the early pioneering work of Descartes who was in fact one of the heroes of the eighteenth-century French radical thinkers, *Les philosophes.*

Enlightenment thought is difficult to characterize briefly. It was a radical intellectual movement with its roots in eighteenth-century northern Europe but became synonymous with philosophical modernity. There is much talk these days of 'the Enlightenment project' as a distinct movement with a clearly identifiable set of aims and objectives. Whatever the Enlightenment is it places great emphasis upon the power of human reason to subvert, expose and overthrow traditional customary practices. There is a fairly direct link between the questioning of the authority of popular wisdom and thought in the *Discourse on Method* and the canonical belief of the Enlightenment that reason should become the litmus test of socially, that is, rationally, acceptable beliefs and activities.

The Enlightenment, in its political crusade to cast aside all bigoted and reactionary forms of thought, which fail the test of reason, has in its sights the dangerous forces of religious and political dogmatism, superstition, prejudice and usurped authority. In other words any legal, religious, moral or political practices, which did not sustain themselves by reason alone, are immediately placed under suspicion as dark forces of reaction. The philosophical tradition, starting with Descartes, gave reason this exalted status and it became a stick to beat ideas and practices, which were taken to be no more than redundant residues of the inherited past.[2]

Placing scientific method and reason together we might call the resulting mixture, giving legitimacy to the modern age, scientific rationality. From it developed the powerful explanatory forces of science and their application, technology. And in the realm of the human sciences they had a pervasive influence on conceptions of

philosophy and politics, inspiring visions of man as a purely rational animal.

We can now return to the problem of method we spoke of at the
beginning of this chapter. Modernity places an uncritical trust in the
power of method to establish self-authenticating truths. The price to
be paid, if it is to be viewed as a tangible loss, is that the ancient
reliance upon textual (and scriptural) authority is placed in doubt
and those customary activities, originally without rational grounds
to sustain them or give them philosophical respectability, are dismissed. Traditional ways of doing things, generally depending upon
customary practices, are anathema to the age of scientific rationality.
So we see, perhaps as a law of the history of philosophy or a general
truth, as one door opens another closes, as scientific rationalism
takes centre stage, customary practices and traditional authorities
(vindicating the authority of ancient texts) are dismissed, discredited
and eventually forgotten.

GADAMER AND METHOD

The history of the development of method and the philosophical
justification, from Descartes to the recent past, provides a vital
context and background to Gadamer's work.[3] Setting his face against
the general current of modernist and Enlightenment thought,
Gadamer questions the status of method and problematizes modernity's over-reliance upon it as a matrix and procedural move in the
quest for indubitable knowledge. The dependence upon rationally
authorized method, for all its progressive and revolutionary benefits –
including the modernist agenda of political liberty and autonomy, the
applications of technology and science to medicine – distances itself
from the world that preceded it. Although the discovery of method
presents something of a radical rupture with the past, the past itself
is, from a certain point of view, always with us and it would be a mistake to forget that the larger formations such as tradition are ever
present and are the appropriate context within which we must place
the seemingly radical, revolutionary and discontinuous. Gadamer
seeks to both question the self-assurance of the modern age and work
towards reinstating aspects of what we have lost when we took on
board all the tenets and beliefs of the Enlightenment. Principally,
what was lost was a harmony, a sense of the world as undivided by the
old and the new, the classical and the ancient, the scholastic and the

modern, but part of a more unitary arrangement, namely, tradition. The establishment of a new method for grounding knowledge must always reconcile itself to the more fundamental force of tradition by which all cultural activity is advanced and maintained. 'Tradition', Gadamer says, 'has a justification that lies beyond rational grounding and in large measure determines our institutions and attitudes' (*TM*, p. 281).

Tradition, and the recent rehabilitation of the notion in cultural and social theory[4] and philosophy, is principally related to its revival in the work of Gadamer. In *Truth and Method* it is a key notion and its importance cannot be overstated.[5] In challenging the supremacy of the Enlightenment it is important to see that the inheritors of this movement did to tradition what Descartes did to his intellectual heritage, the bookish authorities of the past: in both cases they drove a wedge between tradition and reason. The idea that as an unalloyed force and a neutral test, reason can investigate the status and the credentials of tradition is questionable since what we define as rational is always defined within the parameters of tradition. Such a notion of reason would need to stand outside any cultural and historical context. For certain modernist conceptions of reason this kind of move is unproblematic, presupposing an impossible abstraction. However reason is defined, and it is certainly one of the more illusive ideas in philosophy, it has to be located within a specific cultural context, within a certain historical framework. So the Enlightenment dream of a version of reason as a powerful tool for investigating the credentials of tradition is placed in question. In other words, the possibility of exposing all traditions as opposing or wanting in reason is to presuppose that reason and tradition are directly antithetical and mutually exclusive.

Against the idea that tradition stands or falls in the light of an impartial reason, Gadamer looks, in another direction, to the original meaning of tradition. Stemming from the Latin *tradere*, 'to hand on', the word referred to the activity of transmitting, passing something on from generation to generation. There is a way of understanding this transmission as an unreflective action, mindlessly repeated from father to son. But skills and crafts, passed on as part of a tradition, are not merely repeated as on a production line, that which is passed down is constantly in a process of being reworked and reinterpreted. In fact, it makes sense to say that reason, far from being what stands outside tradition as a impartial test, is what is itself handed down in the tradition. Craft activities, as a 'knowing how to', embody the accumulated practical wisdom of the tradition. For Gadamer, tradition is a vital force within culture; it can never be effaced and reduced to a ragbag of non-rational or irrational beliefs since beliefs and rationality themselves are part of wider contexts called tradition. Tradition plays such an important role in Gadamer's work; it is synonymous with that other key element of the everyday world (the 'life world'), language: 'Tradition is not simply a process that experience teaches us to know and govern; it is *language*' (*TM*, p. 358). So to dismiss tradition as the opponent of reason is to miss the point that reason might itself be a feature of tradition. The idea of making tradition an object of investigation wrongly assumes that there is a conceptual and critical space to be found outside tradition, an Archimedean point from which to assess the rationality or otherwise of traditional activities. We can never escape tradition as we are always already within it.

The philosophical consequences of such a view are far reaching and at the heart of Gadamer's work and will be given more detailed treatment when his work on language and interpretation is discussed in Chapter 5. If tradition is an aspect of social life not open to rational investigation then the modernist assumption that method correctly guides one into the disclosure of truth suddenly seems thoroughly questionable.

THE REVIVAL OF TRADITION, AUTHORITY AND PREJUDICE

Modernist thought does not so easily dispense with tradition and the same is the case with the associated pre-Enlightenment ideas, 'authority' and 'prejudice'. Let us first consider Gadamer's treatment of authority.

By what right is something the case, by what entitlement do kings rule, servants serve and words mean whatever they do mean? On whose authority? These are questions we may ask about political practices, the domination of priests and the force of moral practices. It was, no doubt, an assumption of conspiracy-theorist enlighteners that all authority was necessarily usurped and illegitimate if it could not be given the sanction, the imprimatur, of reason. Gadamer comments, 'the concept of authority could be viewed as diametrically opposed to reason and freedom' (*TM*, p. 279). This is not, on the face of it, such a crazy idea; a good deal of authority in social life is underwritten, not by reason but by sometimes arbitrary power and domination. But does this then deny the possibility of the genuine stamp of authority?

For Gadamer, this need not necessarily be the case; in fact authority, genuine authority, carries its own legitimacy: 'Authority . . . properly understood, has nothing to do with blind obedience to commands. Indeed authority has to do not with obedience but knowledge' (*TM*, p. 279). Flying in the face of contemporary theory he looks to the example of pedagogy. Some may argue that the authority of the teacher is no more than an arbitrary social power invested in agents of the state carrying concomitant powers of sanction and punishment. This understanding of authority depends upon one of its many connotations but for Gadamer there is another sense of authority, from which the more modern one has no doubt derived but overshadowed the former sense, that of genuine authority. So a good teacher has authority not by virtue of the sanction of punishment – always to hand if deemed necessary – but for other reasons. Gadamer claims that the genuine authority of the teacher, or any other person in possession of real authority, is not by virtue of the investment of social power but in the ability to open up questions and make certain matters seem crucial, important and worthy of consideration (because they take us to the heart of what we are, within our limited cultural horizons). The real authority of the teacher is in the questions that the inspired educator – more of a Socratic midwife than a dogmatic instructor – makes vivid, vital and important to those in genuine search of knowledge. This is what is meant when it is said that a good teacher carries their own authority; the authority is in the questions they open up and not the sanctions they might bring to bear upon the unruly and the unwilling.

The question of authority is not just about social power and its investment within specific classes and individuals. For Gadamer, it has a strongly philosophical dimension. We can transpose questions of authority to issues surrounding the truthfullness of texts, ideas and writings. Instead of asking whether a philosophical work is true, in the sense of accurately representing reality, we might alternatively enquire into the truthfullness of the questions it raises and seeks to answer. Seen in this light consideration of the authority of a particular text, a particular philosophical text, would not be out of place. Gadamer seeks to demonstrate that it is the *questions* opened up by texts that are somehow more important than the textual producer.

Authority is vested in individuals but its source is 'acknowledgement and knowledge' (*TM*, p. 279). To have authority is to know something and the knowledge is of tradition. This is precisely what Descartes lacked. In his process of doubting everything to establish what could not be placed in doubt he formulated a 'provisional moral code'. But, as Gadamer demonstrates, the provisional moral code is none other than the actually existing system of morality of Descartes's own time. The authority of morality can never be held up to rational scrutiny since what is taken for reason is already defined by the moral code.

Prejudice is in some ways the most important of the trinity, as Gadamer's treatment of it tells us much about his philosophical procedures and commitments. Like tradition and authority, prejudice has suffered distortion at the hands of the enlightenment: 'There is one prejudice of the Enlightenment that defines its essence: the fundamental prejudice of the Enlightenment is the prejudice against prejudice itself' (*TM*, p. 270). Like authority, there is both a positive and negative reading of the term prejudice, and the enlightenment emphasized the negative whilst neglecting the positive. Once again Gadamer seeks to uncover and retrieve submerged meanings of terms encrusted with the prejudices of modernity.

The word prejudice etymologically breaks down into *pre-judice* or *pre*-judgement. Judgement is not possible without the 'pre' that comes before it. All judgements are conditioned by prejudgements. This is an older, pre-modern sense of prejudice Gadamer wants to draw our attention to whereas the familiar understanding of prejudice is unreflective judgement or overhasty reasoning, resulting in the bigotry of purely subjective opinion or the unreflective parroting of purely received wisdom. The point being driven at here is that judgements are made possible not by an abstract and neutral reason but a set of pre-reflective involvements with the world that stand behind judgements and in fact make them possible. A condition of making reflective and evaluative judgements about the world is the possession of prejudices: without prejudgements there can be no judgements. The idea that reflection and judgement depend upon factors other than themselves, that a whole interpreted world is silently, unreflectively, absorbed by the individual in everyday acts of socialization and acculturation, is at the heart of Gadamer's questioning of the enlightenment. What he undermines is the assumption that reason is some kind of matrix and foundation to thought and understanding. Instead of treating rationality as fundamental, a deeper analysis is required to discover what lies behind reason and what make reason itself possible. The turn to this kind of enquiry is made possible by Gadamer's knowledge of the hermeneutical tradition, more especially his mentor Heidegger's use of that tradition which Gadamer takes over and uses in novel and interesting ways.

What the hermeneutical tradition rejects is the idea that a unitary world gives access to a definitive kind of knowledge. Since the time of the ancients this has been the dream of philosophers, and it is nowhere more evident than with the enlightenment, but hermeneutics reveals that all human understanding is ultimately interpretation. A perspective on the world is always just that; it is never an unmediated picture of the way things really are, it is necessarily provisional and limited and can never be a view of the way things really are because the way things really are is as illusory as the philosopher's stone. What we must never forget is that we are always part of what it is we seek to understand: the putative gap between knower and know is more of a fault line or shifting boundary than a chasm.

Gadamer forces us to rethink the fundamental assumptions of the enlightenment. His work goes much against the grain of a good deal of modern (modernist) thought. The view he espouses is part of a general onslaught against the idea of the given, the idea that the world is stable, preformed and somehow more grounded than the conceptual and physical apparatus we possess to apprehend it.

We referred to scientific rationalism as the chief example of methodized thought. The search for correct method is an attempt to overcome the shortcomings of pre-philosophical thought; a dependence upon opinion and purely subjective thinking. Correct method, it is assumed, gives access to the true nature of the world. Descartes's famous example of the wax, as shifting appearance and the wax as it is grasped by pure thought as something unchanging in its essence is a good example of this. The wax as appearance is constantly changing from odourless when cool to fragrant when warmed, solid when cool, malleable and even liquid when heated. But thought, which grasps the real nature of the wax, finds its secret and hidden essence to be fixed and unchanging. This example gives a model of science. The thoughts, opinions, perceptions and bodily attributes of the individual give access to nothing more than shifting and uncertain appearances; these aspects of the individual are nothing more than distractions from the pursuit of pure knowledge. But what this account of science tends to forget is that the investigator or experimenter is a part of what it is they are experimenting upon. No matter how careful one is about the method used to investigate the world, one must always remember that the world is being seen from a particularly human framework and dimension. Kant's realization that space and time and the categories are what individuals contribute to our understanding of the world and that the world is not given but in part constructed (or constituted) by human thought is now taken for granted by many philosophers. This Kantian realization that all knowledge is ultimately human knowledge, knowledge from a specifically human perception, raises the important philosophical question of the relationship between subjects and objects. The dream of science is to abolish the specificity of the subject and the generality of the culture of the investigator, and focus upon an assumed universality common to all subjects. For Descartes that universality is reason and the application of a method that, whatever the variations in language, culture, history, and so forth, will always yield the same results and solutions. What has this to do with the myth of the Given? It assumes that reason will give access to that universality that transcends the particularity of time and place. If the Given is questionable how then must we proceed if we are to attain knowledge? If the subject is invariably a part of the picture does this not make all knowledge subjective? This is a crucial question Gadamer's work confronts. The answer from the perspective of philosophical hermeneutics is that subjects and objects are indivisible.

The myth of the Given assumes that there is a world out there to be discovered if only we could find the right method we could find something like an 'Open sesame!' a way of unlocking the hidden treasure. The whole modern dependence upon scientific rationalism goes back a long way in the history of philosophy. The gap between subjects and objects is like the gap between appearance and reality, and the most important gap of all, that between thought and the world. Since Plato, on one reading of the history of philosophy, thought seeks to accurately replicate the world. In fact here the point of philosophy is to reproduce the world in thought. This depends upon a certain view of thought and language which takes it to be principally mimetic, representative and designative in nature. Is language a way of replicating the world? On the myth of the Given, language describes a pre-existing world. But is it possible to conceive the matter the other way round? Could we not say that without language there is no world? Or put another way, could we not say that language constitutes the world rather than describes it? Language is also taken to be the silent medium through which thoughts travel. On this view thought precedes language; in fact there would be no language if there was not first thought to, as it were, make itself manifest in speech.

Once again it is possible to reverse the polarity here and think about the possibility of language preceding thought. Is it so absurd to suggest that thought is nothing more than internalized speech? I would say that it is in fact more plausible than the idea that thought comes first which is then translated into speech. What is a wordless thought like? What is a thought that cannot be put into words; what is its status and how is it to be understood and communicated? To make thought prior to speech ends up in all sorts of dead ends and problems. There is a whole tradition in philosophy which rejects the orthodoxy of the supremacy of thought and reason. In this tradition, in the modern period starting with Hamann, language encompasses everything. Language is not taken to be a means of communication principally. Language is a form of expression. What makes language possible is not the representing relationship between word and object but the idea that language is principally expressive. It expresses a way of life (Wittgenstein's 'form of life').

All of this is by way of an introduction to Gadamer. The legacy of scientific rationalism, and the various philosophical positions it depends upon, are fraught with difficulties. The very status and existence of the human sciences is under threat. Truth as a product of infallible method ignores truths of experience enshrined within a common cultural tradition. This is all by way of a prelude to the positive dimension to his work. This is to show how truth is never to be methodized. Neither is it is something we finally arrive at and achieve. All our activities in the social world are 'on the way to' truth but it is never finally achieved.

To recapitulate, Gadamer questions the foundations of the Enlightenment; more specifically he rejects its dependence upon a conception of method acquired from procedures of natural science. Method, as conceived by the modern age, overshadows elements of wisdom and understanding about the world. Invariably more practical than theoretical, the forms of understanding effaced by method can be reclaimed as aspects of authority, prejudice and tradition. However, the notions of authority, prejudice and tradition need to be seen not as obstacles and impediments to liberating reason but as vehicles of reason and liberation themselves.

This chapter has introduced some of the most important ideas in Gadamer's work. It also gives some insight into his way of proceeding. Taking concepts and scrutinizing them not simply as logical but as historical and philological categories is revealing. As witnessed with authority, prejudice and tradition, Gadamer lets these terms speak again by disclosing the hidden and submerged nuances of meanings the modern age has sought to silence. With this in mind it is tempting to ask the following question. If Gadamer is just interested in the meanings of words is he not like an analytic philosopher whose task is to clarify meanings by attention to the way we use words? But Gadamer's procedure is more philological than logical. In attending to linguistic variations he is drawing upon language within cultural and historical contexts, and showing the wider implications, for philosophy and interpretation, of these contexts. He is not re-evaluating notions of authority, prejudice and tradition, simply to bring to light lost meanings; he is offering a critique of philosophical modernity. And as well as a critique of modernity he presents an alternative perspective with far-reaching consequences for philosophy. Consistent with his position the alternative is not a radically new system of philosophy; it is simply a retrieval of a way of understanding everyday thought and experience that has been marginalized, ironically, by the tradition. This alternative he calls hermeneutics, or more specifically philosophical hermeneutics. Hermeneutics, the art of interpretation, is Greek in origin but, Gadamer argues, it is at the heart of all forms of understanding and represents a radical riposte to a view of the world regulated by method. Hermeneutics best describes our relationship to the world but, because of a fog of modernist thought where everything is defined within the limits of method, we are unable to realize alternatives.

Hermeneutics, when seen as a way of being in the world, is the most primordial form of understanding. We are not subjects grasping objects but 'hermeneutical' beings within tradition. But hermeneutics, the well-established practice of interpreting texts, is a different but related matter. Its history and development needs to be traced from the rise of biblical, literary and legal hermeneutics in the seventeenth and eighteenth centuries to the twentieth century to see that even hermeneutics becomes tainted and the sense of 'hermeneutical' Gadamer advocates needs rescuing from the clutches of modernist thought. To achieve this Gadamer turns to the work of Heidegger whose radical reworking of hermeneutics provides the inspiration for philosophical hermeneutics.

NOTES

1 The full title in French is *Discours de la Méthode pour bien conduire sa raison, et chercher la vérité dans les sciences. Plus la Dioptrique, les Météores et la Géométrie qui sont des essais de cette Méthode.* And in English: *Discourse on the Method of rightly conducting one's reason and seeking the truth in the sciences, and in addition the Optics, the Meteorology, and the Geometry, which are essays in this Method.*
2 Although his work was an inspiration to Enlightenment thought, Descartes did not share the virulent anti-clericalism of his successors although his piety often seems more strategic, a ruse for not offending the Holy Office, than heartfelt.
3 As we will see presently Gadamer is by no means alone in his critique of Descartes and his legacy; in fact almost every philosopher in the twentieth century started out from a critique of Descartes.
4 The sociological work of Edward Shils, and more recently that of Anthony Giddens, comes to mind here.
5 Tradition becomes less important in Gadamer's work after *Truth and Method*, being superseded by the more morally and politically charged notion of 'solidarity' as a more appropriate description of the binding force at the heart of social life.

CHAPTER 3

FROM HERMENEUTICS TO PHILOSOPHICAL HERMENEUTICS

WHAT IS HERMENEUTICS?

The previous chapter presents a sketch of the modern age by seeking to show how its reliance upon a well-grounded method gives rise to the dominance of scientific rationalism. Apart from its efficacy in the realm of scientific discovery and technology, *such rationalism* overshadows and forecloses alternative paths to truth and understanding. To contest the hegemony of philosophical modernity Gadamer turns to hermeneutics, the art of interpretation, and forges from this relatively limited textual practice, philosophical hermeneutics, a profound challenge to much that theoretically underpins what I term 'philosophical modernity'.

In this chapter the voyage from ancient hermeneutics to Gadamer's individual philosophical hermeneutics is charted. The *locus classicus* in his work for this account is *Truth and Method*. In *Truth and Method*, subtitled 'Elements of a Philosophical Hermeneutics', Gadamer lays out a philosophical hermeneutics by means of the thought that all aspects of human understanding presuppose a hermeneutical dimension; in this sense hermeneutics is universal. Hermeneutics is not yet another method to replace an already existing one; on the contrary Gadamer turns to hermeneutics because he sees in it a form of repressed knowledge and understanding abruptly curtailed by the procedures of modernity. Part of Gadamer's mission in *Truth and Method* is to let the hermeneutical dimension to truth speak out once again; in order to do this he devises a narrative to account for the changing fortunes of hermeneutical practice. The narrative starts in the early eighteenth century with the hermeneutical techniques devised for correct interpretation of the Bible. On

Gadamer's account hermeneutics eventually falls victim to the siren voices of modernity and finds itself embroiled in the question of methodology. This has the effect of undermining hermeneutics by placing it in direct competition with science: a competition it is bound to lose. But the result is not complete surrender. Gadamer finds a way to revive hermeneutics and rescue it from the clutches of the epistemological concerns of method by following Martin Heidegger's so-called 'hermeneutics of facticity'.

ROMANTIC HERMENEUTICS

The term hermeneutics, meaning an interpretation of a certain kind of aesthetic text, is used much these days in relation to literary theory. In fact the term is in danger of overuse, to such an extent that 'interpretation' and 'hermeneutic' are synonymous. There are important differences, as a brief survey of the concept's history will reveal. The term goes back to classical antiquity and has a more limited denotation. The Greek term *hermeneuein*, meaning to interpret, is the root from which the word hermeneutics is derived. For the Greeks interpretation was the elucidation and explication of elusive sacred messages and signs. Herme – the name is associated with *hermeneuein* – the messenger of the Gods, interpreted the wishes of the deities making their desires known to mere mortals. Developing out of this idea of making the ways of God known to man, Protestant theology of the seventeenth century, wishing to understand scripture in a more systematic and less allegorical fashion, devised *hermeneutica*, an 'art' of interpretation with its own procedures and techniques. The standard view was that if the Bible was the word of God, divine revelation, it should be interpreted authentically and standards of correct procedure should be devised to expedite the task. Early hermeneutic strategies only came into play when the biblical text seemed opaque and resisted easy translation and explanation. Understanding was taken to be the rule rather than the exception and thus hermeneutical strategies only became necessary when the text lapsed into mysteriousness or became incomprehensible and the pitfalls of misunderstanding were evident.

Key figures in the development of early modern hermeneutics are J. C. Dannhauser,[1] the rationalist philosopher Benedict Spinoza,[2] Friedrich Ast, Chladenius and Friedrich August Wolf. They devised rules for the accurate interpretation of biblical, legal and classical texts. These figures may be the founding fathers of modern hermeneutics but it was Friedrich Schleiermacher (1768–1834), the German philosopher and theologian, whose work was to have the biggest impact in the development of Romantic hermeneutics. For Schleiermacher the ancient hermeneutical principle that we can more readily ascribe understanding than misunderstanding to a text was mistaken. Misunderstanding was always a possibility even with the most accessible of texts. It is misguided to assume that misunderstandings are limited to difficult and opaque words and phrases the reader encounters: the danger of misunderstanding is a feature of all interpretation. Understanding is not to be taken for granted but must be searched out and willed. The move from textual interpretation to the more general question of the nature of understanding is central to an assessment of Schleiermacher's achievement. With Schleiermacher it is not only texts that warrant interpretation, it is a feature of all modes of understanding. The problem of understanding is not confined to foreign and ancient languages, nor does it simply pertain to biblical text. It extends to the speaker's native language, whether one wants to make sense of the language of one's own past or the present; for hermeneutics, both instances confront the problem of understanding. One may refer to a regional or a specific hermeneutics in so far as there were differing procedures for the interpretation of different kinds of texts (as we have already mentioned, biblical, legal and classical literary and philosophical texts). Schleiermacher's principal achievement was to devise a general hermeneutics, a procedure applicable to all forms of interpretation.[3] Important are the various writings collected in the volume *Hermeneutics and Criticism and other writings*[4] and the celebrated 'Aphorisms on Hermeneutics'.[5]

Schleiermacher alludes to the 'hermeneutic circle' as a puzzle at the heart of interpretation. The idea of the circle is not unique to hermeneutics as it featured in classical rhetoric but Schleiermacher gives the circle emphasis and makes it the heart of his theory of interpretation. Here is one of his many formulations of the circle:

> There is . . . an opposition between the unity of the whole and the individual parts of the work, so that the task could be set in a twofold manner, namely to understand the unity of the whole by the individual parts and the value of the individual parts via the unity of the whole.[6]

This is a classic statement of the hermeneutic circle. The whole is to be understood in the relationship to the parts, and the parts the whole. A good way of illustrating the hermeneutic circle is to think about the activity of reading a novel. When reading one is always anticipating a total meaning in the text; the resolution of narrative conflicts, the working out of the story and so forth. The reader always has in mind a desire to make all of the individual parts of the text fit together by anticipating the book's overall meaning. The meaning of the book is seen as unfolding and the end of the book is its resolution. At the same time as anticipating a totalized meaning one is always in the process of reading one small part of the work; first a word, then a sentence, then a paragraph. These parts of the work contribute to the total meaning of the work so one can speak here of a constant movement between parts and whole. The signification of the words in a text are not to be taken in isolation but as a unit of meaning that is constantly in the process of modification in relation to the implied total meaning of the text. This illustration of the hermeneutic circle in operation in the process of reading is not Schleiermacher's but it gives some insight into the idea that textual meaning is best understood as a dynamic transaction between part and whole. There is actually a puzzle here. The mysterious part–whole affiliation haunts every kind of interpretation. In fact more than a conundrum we have what in conventional logical terms looks to be a straightforward fallacy. Part and whole seem to be mutually exclusive and logically incompatible. To make matters more difficult Schleiermacher not only readily accepts the circle but also sees it constantly expanding. Michael Inwood has described this well.

> At each level of interpretation we are involved in a hermeneutical circle. We cannot know the correct reading of a passage in a text unless we know, roughly, the text as a whole; we cannot know the text as a whole unless we know particular passages. We cannot know the meaning of a word unless we know the meanings of the surrounding words and of the text as a whole; knowing the meaning of the whole involves knowing the meaning of individual words. We cannot fully understand the text unless we know the author's life and works as a whole, but this requires knowledge of the texts and other events that constitute his life. We cannot fully understand a text unless we know about the whole

culture from which it emerged, but this presupposes a knowledge of the texts and so on that constitute the culture.[7]

Schleiermacher extends interpretation beyond semantic meanings of the text to the broad cultural and historical meanings, which give the text context. On this account meaning is relative to context. The charge that the hermeneutic circle violates the principles of formal logic only sticks if one sees meanings as fixed. When meanings are understood to be constantly redefined in relation to shifting contexts the circularity is no longer vicious.

One aspect of the hermeneutic circle is the gap between the author's thought processes, beliefs, intentions and the commonly understood meanings of the words used. This space between word meaning and authorial intention and speaker meaning gives rise to the central distinction in Schleiermacher between the *grammatical* and the *psychological* types of interpretation. The grammatical or linguistic refers to interpretation at the level of syntactical meaning and the rules of grammar, and the psychological form of interpretation at the level of authorial intention. Michael Foster explains Schleiermacher's distinction as follows:

> Interpretation proper always has two sides: one linguistic, the other psychological. Linguistic interpretation's task . . . consists in inferring from the evidence consisting in particular actual uses of words to the rules that are governing them, i.e. to their usages and thus to their meanings; psychological interpretation instead focuses on an author's psychology. Linguistic interpretation is mainly concerned with what is common or shared in a language; psychological interpretation mainly with what is distinctive to a particular author.[8]

The suggestion is that we need to understand language from both directions. The *grammatical* interpretation is given via a grasp of the meanings in common usage. The *psychological* interpretation goes beyond this; it refers to nuances not captured by grammatical interpretation. If someone says, 'This is a fine country!' it is impossible to interpret, at the purely grammatical level, whether the utterance is said sincerely, humorously, ironically, bitterly or resentfully. This list of attributes moves beyond the grammatical to the psychological in that these qualities go beyond the actual statement to say something about the character of the utterer, which in turn enriches the context for interpretation.

In *Truth and Method* Gadamer regards Schleiermacher's turn to a general hermeneutics as a key move in the history of hermeneutics. On the other hand he is critical of the path Schleiermacher treads, particularly around the whole question of psychological interpretation. At issue is the notion of reconstruction. For Gadamer, Schleiermacher sees interpretation as a reconstruction of the state of mind of the author. This entails what he terms 'divination', that is, 'placing oneself within the whole framework of the author, an apprehension of the "inner origin" of the composition of a work, a recreation of a creative act' (*TM*, p. 187). Whereas grammatical interpretation deals with established linguistic meanings, psychological interpretation stays at the level of individuality. In the act of divination the interpreter sets out to disclose the meaning of a play or a poem, say, by seeking to re-create the unique state of mind of the author in the moment of artistic creation. Interpretation on this account amounts to getting into the head of the creative artist to reconstruct the assumed intentions and inspirations motivating a particular work. The real point of romantic hermeneutics, says Gadamer, echoing Schleiermacher himself, is 'to understand a writer better than he understood himself' (*TM*, p. 192). As well as seeing a work in its historical context, as well as locating it within an established genre, the real hermeneutical task is to uncover the artist's uniqueness, the artist's ability to go beyond the readily classifiable, and this takes the interpreter into the psychology of genius.

For Gadamer, although he readily concurs with the thought that interpretation goes well beyond the self-understanding of the author, sees in Schleiermacher's hermeneutics a series of wrong turns diminishing the importance of his central insight that the hermeneutical problem has universal application extending to written and spoken, ancient and foreign, languages. Against this, the stress upon psychological interpretation has the following regrettable consequences: an overemphasis upon the subjectivity of the author and, following from this, the subordination of the text and its meaning to conjecture by the interpreter concerning the author's psychology. Let us look at these aspects one by one. The process of divination, and the attention to psychological interpretation, has the effect of overemphasizing the role of the author and his/her genius, on Gadamer's reading of Schleiermacher. Gadamer strongly suggests that the problem here is that divination becomes a formula or method, neglecting the productive role of the interpreter. For Gadamer, the process of understanding a text is not achieved by making the interpreter invisible in the face of the author's psychology; it results from the 'oscillating movement between part and whole' (*TM*, p. 191). In other words, hermeneutical understanding, as it exits for Gadamer, is more dialogical and interactive, depending on a collective version of understanding, not one that focuses on the sole interpreter in the face of the text. He says, 'the ultimate ground of all understanding must always be a divinatory act of congeniality, the possibility of which depends upon a pre-existing bond between individuals' (*TM*, p. 189). The idea of dialogue, made possible by the 'pre-existing bonds', cannot be overemphasized in Gadamer, as we will come to realize in later chapters, and it is the absence of the interactive dialogue between text and interpreter, whole and parts, past and present, that sustains part of the critical attitude to Schleiermacher. Gadamer claims (of Schleiermacher), 'he regards texts, independently of their claim to truth, as purely expressive phenomena' (*TM*, p. 196). No doubt a text, especially a literary text, is both expressive and makes some sort of claim about the world. Gadamer accuses Schleiermacher of focusing on the expressive dimension of language, the power, that is, of the literary artist to express his or her own vision, without having regard for the power of language itself to disclose truth. The truthfulness of a text, for Gadamer, is its power to throw light on fundamental 'matters at issue'. These are never made explicit in Gadamer but the assumption is that every culture is preoccupied with the fundamental existential issues of death and life and every tradition opens up its own way of expressing truth about these matters at issue, or fundamental concerns. The whole question of truth is important in Gadamer, as the title of his major work, *Truth and Method*, makes clear. We will defer detailed discussion of Gadamer's account of truth until Chapters 4, 5 and 6.

Gadamer's principal critique of Schleiermacher revolves around his distinction between the grammatical and the psychological forms of interpretation and a perceived prioritizing of the psychological over the grammatical. A good deal of modern scholarship has come to question Gadamer's tendentious reading of Schleiermacher and have more or less accused him of distorting his account of this chapter in the history of hermeneutics to make his own narrative appear the more plausible. In defence of Schleiermacher the distance between the grammatical and the psychological is never as emphatic as Gadamer makes it. The insinuation that Schleiermacher commits the 'intentionalist fallacy', the fallacy of judging a text or a work of art purely in terms of the intentions of the author/artist, is unsustainable. The psychological feature Schleiermacher alludes to are made manifest in language, that is, via grammatical interpretation. It is really the text that one focuses on even for evidence of the psychological trace of the author.

Essentially Gadamer's snapshot of the history of hermeneutics, as presented in *Truth and Method*, aims to show how that history is subverted by the quest for method, bringing nineteenth-century hermeneutics close to the more obviously methodized enterprise, science. It takes the work of Wilhelm Dilthey, and eventually Martin Heidegger, to liberate hermeneutics from its methodological straitjacket. The task to be performed is to show how understanding is ultimately historical. It is only once this path has been trodden that philosophical hermeneutics can come into its own.

DILTHEY'S HERMENEUTICS

After Schleiermacher the most significant figure in the development of hermeneutics is his biographer, the German philosopher and social thinker Wilhelm Dilthey (1833–1911). Dilthey is a central figure in the debates in the nineteenth century concerning the nature and status of science and he was to have a profound effect upon the future development of hermeneutics, especially upon the work of Heidegger and Gadamer. Against one prevailing tendency to collapse all knowledge into a broad category of science, Dilthey saw knowledge as having two distinct component parts, these being the natural sciences and the human sciences (the *Geisteswissenschaften*); natural science being the activity we ordinarily understand as science, the hard science of cause and effect. The human sciences were all those branches of knowledge concerned with understanding the practicalities of human life such as economics, history and philosophy. Dilthey also included the most creative aspects of humanity which in their own way were an expression of life, these being art and literature. We often refer to these as the arts or the humanities. For Dilthey, what divides these two basic categories of knowledge is their objective. In the case of natural science the point is to provide explanations. But causal explanation is inappropriate to the human sciences; what is needed here is understanding, *Verstehen*, rather than straightforward empirical description and explanation. Dilthey warns against the dangers of applying the methodologies of natural science, albeit very successful methodologies for explaining and describing the causal connections between things in the natural world, to strictly human activities. Even Aristotle, in the opening methodological section of his *Nicomachean Ethics*, advises caution for those expecting the kind of precision and exactness of science in the study of human affairs. Given the complexity and unpredictability of social life – the elementary fact that we are all in some sense unique and different – we must make do with things that are for the most part true. So what kind of truths can we legitimately expect to gain from a study of the human sciences? More than this, the problem with any study of human life is that we are always part of what it is we are seeking to understand. This raises special difficulties that are not immediately obvious in natural science because the ideals of detachment and impartiality are more readily identifiable with the study of empirical data. The sense in which, for Gadamer, Dilthey is an advance on Schleiermacher is his move away from psychological interpretation, away from the focus upon subjective meanings and a move towards the broader category of 'life'. Since Feuerbach and Nietzsche there is a movement in philosophy which prioritizes the category of life over reflection and reason, taking cognitive qualities to be an integral part of life and not uniquely separate qualities. Philosophical attempts to make sense of man and the world from a theoretical and rational standpoint are criticized because philosophical reflection ignores the pre-philosophical thought of the 'life world' and hence does violence to our everyday relationships in the world. We are involved in the world and find our way around in it long before we start to philosophize. In fact the philosophical perspective on life is a distortion depending on forms of thought unrelated to the real character of human relationships in the world.

For Dilthey the human studies are in themselves part of the attempt to understand the world at the level of lived experience. Whose lived experience? Here Dilthey evokes a version of the hermeneutic circle. Understandings of the life world in the present are always hermeneutically linked to the cultural past which is the history of the human sciences and studies made manifest in the cultural and textual artefacts of the past. For Dilthey hermeneutical understanding is inextricably connected to the past. The category of life shows that interpretations in the present are always linked to the history of those interpretations in the past. We are irredeemably historical. Even though Schleiermacher thought of interpretation as a task involving some measure of historical reconstruction he failed to stress the thought that all understanding has a necessarily historical dimension. This was Dilthey's foremost contribution to hermeneutics. Despite the turn to historical understanding Dilthey's work was to be criticized by subsequent thinkers including Gadamer, as we shall see.

Although Dilthey was able to account for the differences between the natural and the human sciences and show how the human sciences were hermeneutical and not like natural science involved in explanation, he was too much a product of his time and was unable to free himself from the strictures of a quest for method. Dilthey believed in the possibility of acquiring objectively valid knowledge, even if it was intrinsically historical and interpretive. The move towards a historical hermeneutics, that is, a hermeneutics that stresses the link in understanding between past and present, is a crucial turn as it is a key source of inspiration for Gadamer's mentor, Heidegger.

HEIDEGGER'S 'HERMENEUTICS OF FACTICITY'

The phenomenological and existential thinker Martin Heidegger is a key figure in the history of the development of hermeneutics. Although he refrained from mentioning hermeneutics in his later work, his early 1927 masterpiece *Being and Time* is both strongly influenced by hermeneutics and the analysis of human existence (*Dasein*), depends upon a radical redirection of the hermeneutic circle.[9] More importantly for our purposes, it is Heidegger's revolutionary reorientation of hermeneutics that is so important for appreciating the future direction of Gadamer's thought. On Gadamer's reading Dilthey's appreciation of the historical nature of understanding was still linked to a methodological perspective on the human sciences – despite his absorption of the category of life. For Gadamer, it is Heidegger who genuinely revealed the historicity of understanding and liberated hermeneutics from its connection to the search for a method parallel to the natural sciences.

In *Truth and Method* Gadamer explores a key section of Heidegger's *Being and Time*. Gadamer analyses the significance of the hermeneutic circle for Heidegger as a prelude to his own appropriation of the position.

> It is not to be reduced to the level of a vicious circle, or even a circle which is merely tolerated. In the circle is hidden a positive possibility of the most primordial kind of knowing, and we genuinely grasp this possibility only when we have understood that out first, last, and constant task in interpreting is never to allow our fore-having, fore-sight, and fore-conception to be presented to us by fancies and popular conceptions, but rather to make the scientific theme secure by working out these fore-structures in terms of the things themselves.[10]

The real clue to the hermeneutic circle is the cluster of pre-existing interpretations that make other interpretations possible. Heidegger's basic point is that before we can actually interpret the world we need to be aware of the fact that certain things cannot themselves be interpreted subjectively as they are those very things on which interpretations depend. Heidegger speaks of a 'fore-having, fore-sight, and fore-conception'. This is, on the face of it, a very odd assertion. It seems as though we need to have before we have, see before we see and conceive before we conceive. In a sense this is precisely what Heidegger has in mind. The Cartesian thought that we can introspect and give our knowledge absolute foundations because everything that cannot be doubted must logically then be beyond doubt is a flawed project. It assumes that thinking is a kind of transparent medium. Against this idea Heidegger seeks to show that the conditions that make thought itself possible are not self-generated but are put in place long before we engage in acts of introspection. A way of revealing the shortcomings of Descartes's whole project of introspective doubt can be seen in this remark from Ludwig Wittgenstein's *On Certainty* when he asks himself: 'Can I be making a mistake . . . in thinking that the words of which this sentence is composed are English words whose meaning I know?'[11] Descartes imagines that he can legitimately doubt everything except the process of doubting or thinking that comes to light in the assertion of the cogito argument. What the Wittgenstein remark suggests, almost wittingly contra Descartes, is that one cannot, for example, doubt that the language one is using to express doubt is itself doubtful. What would it be to think that I might be mistaken about the language I am now using to express the thought that

I might he mistaken? Wittgenstein's point, it seems, is that certain doubts make no sense. More than this, he appears to be showing us that a condition of genuine doubt is that certain things cannot be doubted. Or expressed another way, before we start to doubt things via language we need to be mindful of the fact that certain things are beyond doubt. Certain things need to be in place before doubting can proceed: we engage with the world in a practical sense long before we seek to reflect upon it. Wittgenstein's remark is a very Heideggerian thought in that it brings out the fore-having, in this case of language. Again the Wittgenstein quote reveals that there are certain things about our relationship to the world, which cannot be placed in doubt and cannot be legitimately taken as an object of investigation. We cannot divorce ourselves from the language we speak to inquire into its true nature or ask whether the language we speak is really all that we take it to be. There has to be an implicit engagement with language, a tacit relationship to a linguistic world, before we can ask specific meaningful questions within it.

There needs to be some sense of the world before we can start to make judgements about it: in fact we are already involved in the world long before we detach ourselves from the world theoretically to seek to understand it philosophically. Heidegger is challenging a version of the 'myth of the Given' here. We do not come into the world a *tabula rasa* and over time develop a sense of the world as coherent and continuous and open to rational thought. We start from practical involvements in the world, activities and forms of socialization. These are, described differently, the fore-conceptions, fore-havings and fore-sights. Through cultural training we unreflectively inherit a world-view, a perspective upon the world. Of course these are by no means complete and exhaustive being the starting points from which we endeavour to make our individual interpretations of the world. However, we can now see the way in which Heidegger has appropriated the hermeneutic circle. There is a version of the part/whole circle in operation in the everyday understandings of the world. There is, as it were, a background understanding, implicit and unstated, constantly in play, which works in tandem with what we might call the foreground understanding, that is, everything open to reflection, judgement, interpretation. Heidegger exposes the hermeneutical structure at the heart of existence.

Dasein, Heidegger's own terminology for human existence, finds its way around the world of its own creating by understanding it. But everyday understanding is not reflective; it might even be helpful to think of it as what is under where we stand, and yet what can never be made an object of full, conscious, understanding. With everyday understanding we take up a relationship to the world and unwittingly adopt a mode of being which Heidegger calls 'hermeneutic'. The world is interpreted 'as' a particular world wherein is the 'positive possibility of the most primordial kind of knowing'. It is hermeneutic because Dasein, through its practical involvements in the already culturally interpreted world, is ceaselessly projecting into the future whilst rooted in tacit understandings in the present and the past. Human existence is not trapped in the fore-understandings because they are the condition on which we seek to understand the world in a more explicit self-conscious way. Heidegger contrasts the hermeneutic 'as' with the apophantic 'as'. The hermeneutic 'as' – on the basis of our practical involvements with the world, our behaviour – expresses our relationship to the world at some basic level. We are constantly interpreting as we 'predicatively' engage in projects. In other words we are always interpreting the world, even before we attempt some kind of philosophical understanding of it. For this reason, Heidegger sees the 'apophantic' or 'propositional' 'as' as derivative. The apophantic 'as' is the world seen through language, which for Heidegger is actually dependent upon a more primordial 'as' of hermeneutical interpretation. His famous example is, 'The hammer is heavy'. If we refer to the hammer 'as' heavy we are using logical categories to define its mode of being and we seek to capture something essential about the hammer in its heaviness. However, a more authentic disclosure of the hammer takes place when it is mislaid and its activity as a tool is fractured and disrupted. The reality of the hammer, its activity in the life context of a blacksmith say, is concealed until the tool is no longer evident. Its authentic existence is not as an object to be described and categorized but as a tool within a context of equipment and within a wider context of a world of work.

Once again Heidegger is resisting the myth of the Given. The pre-predicative is given in that it is there before we come to reflect upon it. We have this fundamental relationship to the world which is practical and engaged; our knowledge is more of the practical 'knowing how to' variety than the more cognitive 'knowing that'. A purely theoretical attitude to the world, in the manner of Descartes and subsequent philosophers, may be possible but it must not be taken to be fundamental. It depends upon a more basic relationship to the world. The hermeneutical circle is the interpretive projection of Dasein upon the world in the form of individual projects and activities and the background fore-structure that informs the projects and is in constant movement with them.

In discussing Heidegger's turn to hermeneutics Jean Grondin sums up his achievement in the following way:

> Hermeneutics . . . is to be taken in the 'primordial signification of the word, where it designates the business of interpreting'. This understanding of the term rejects the view, dominant since Schleiermacher and Dilthey, that hermeneutics is an art or technique of understanding, the purpose of which is to constrict a methodological foundation for the human sciences. Not theory of interpretation but interpretation itself is the subject matter of a hermeneutics that is to achieve the status of philosophy.[12]

The move away from theory of interpretation to interpretation itself is a move to practical activity. There is a constant and ever-present hermeneutical movement in the structure of understanding within everyday life and it is the starting point for Gadamer's hermeneutics. Traditional hermeneutics, up to the end of the eighteenth century, was a technique for correctly interpreting sacred and secular texts and the law. Starting with Schleiermacher and working through Dilthey and Heidegger, hermeneutics becomes not just a way of reading and understanding texts but a description of the nature of human understanding itself. The circular dynamic between part and whole becomes a way of describing the (pre-philosophical) structure of everyday human understanding. Experience, thought and language are hermeneutical in the sense that they involve a constant dynamic between the fore-conceptions, which are grounded not in nature but culture, and interpretation. Together they comprise tradition, which is not just the inert past but also a dialogue between past, present and future. In the next chapter we will see how understanding is necessarily a dialogue. A dialogue with another in pursuit of understanding, and a common dialogue with the past as all interpretations in the present necessarily encounter, most significantly through language, the echoes of the past in tradition. To say all understanding is ultimately interpretation is a sentiment with which Gadamer concurs. As he says, 'We are indebted to German romanticism for disclosing the systematic significance of the verbal nature of conversation for all understanding. It has taught us that understanding and interpretation are ultimately the same thing' (*TM*, p. 388).

NOTES

1 His principal work is *Hermeneutica sacra sive methodus exponendarum sacrarum litterarum* (1654).
2 *Tractatus theologico-politicus* (1670).
3 '*Hermeneutics as* the art of understanding *does not yet exist* in a general manner, *there are instead only several forms* of specific hermeneutics' (Schleiermacher, 1998, p. 5).
4 See Schleiermacher (1998). The volume consists of a variety of Schleiermacher's writings on hermeneutics.
5 See Ormiston and Schrift (1990), pp. 57–84.
6 Schleiermacher (1998), p. 109.
7 See Michael Inwood's entry on 'Hermeneutics' in Craig and Floridi (1998).
8 Foster (2002).
9 Richard Palmer interestingly points out that although Heidegger effectively turns his back on hermeneutics and only infrequently uses the term in his work after *Being and Time*, '[He] turns increasingly to reinterpreting earlier philosophers – Kant, Nietzsche, Hegel – and the poetry of Rilke, Trakl and Hölderlin. His thinking becomes more "hermeneutical" in the traditional sense of being centred on text interpretation' (1969, p. 126).
10 Quoted in *TM*, p. 266.
11 Wittgenstein (1969), # 158.
12 Grondin (1994), p. 98.

CHAPTER 4

TRUTH WITHOUT METHOD

GADAMER AND TRUTH

The analysis so far has been rather negative focusing on what Gadamer rejects as the legacy of the Enlightenment. The principal idea of method and its influence even upon hermeneutical thought was the object of criticism. Heidegger's existential reading of the hermeneutical circle provides the real starting point of Gadamer's own contribution to modern thought. To get a sense of this we need to return briefly to Heidegger. Heidegger's existential hermeneutics, stressing the fore-structure of understanding, has many radical consequences for traditional conceptions, not the least of which is a re-definition of truth, or rather a revival of a more fundamental version of truthfulness.

Gadamer following Heidegger rejects the orthodox account of truth as correspondence, representation or, as it came to be known, adequation. However, we have yet to see what positive account of truth Gadamer is willing to affirm and what substantive positions he advances in his major work, *Truth and Method*. Gadamer's account of truth is an important area of concern, not least because his major work includes it in the title. As we will see, Gadamer has surprisingly little to say about truth as ordinarily understood in philosophical theory[1] and yet its inclusion in the title of his work is justified since an unorthodox understanding of truth is at the heart of his overall project.

The most familiar account of truth, where it is regarded as a correspondence between a knowing subject and a known object, goes back to Plato.[2] At its most basic it affirms an exact correspondence between human perception of the world and the way the world actually is. An account of something is true on this theory if mind and its object match up in some coherent way. Regulating correspondence is the thought that one can have an unmediated, undistorted apprehension of the way things really are because the mind is an infallible guide to truths about the external world. Modern empiricists and rationalists, from different perspectives, claim undistorted access to the reality of objects via strategies of correspondence. Although the notion of correspondence goes back to classical antiquity and medieval scholasticism, it endures well into modernity and is still a well-established idea in much modern epistemology. The problem, as Gadamer states it, is that the true becomes entangled with philosophical theories of truth – such as correspondence – and their aspirations to objectivity. One of Gadamer's central claims is that *method occludes truth* or rather that a basic and fundamental encounter with truth is lost once we resort to a dependence upon method. Gadamer's key work could just as easily have been *Truth or Method* as *Truth and Method*. There is an inexhaustible tension between the two if truth is taken to be the end product of method.

Following on from earlier considerations of method and its fallibility, even truth, as it is theorized in modernity, is in danger of covering up more fundamental truths. It is these other dimensions of truth that Gadamer seeks to disclose in *Truth and Method*. Far from being marginal or unimportant they offer experiences of truth from which philosophical theories of truth are merely derivative. The structure of *Truth and Method* as three large sections is actually based around the three basic experiences of truth: art, historical understanding and language.[3] For Gadamer, these are not to be understood as theories, far from it, they are encounters with truth. Part of his argument is to rescue these experiences of truth from truth as correspondence, which in turn means rescuing them from the tradition's misappropriation of them through method.

The experience of art in modernity becomes known as aesthetics in the eighteenth century and truth is replaced by feeling. Historical understanding, that is, experiencing one's place within a living tradition, becomes methodized historical science, and language, the truth of which is experienced everyday and also exists in its most rarefied form in literary language, is reduced to an alienated abstraction, the philosophy of language. *Truth and Method* aims to show how the revealed truths of all of these modes of understanding can be reclaimed and revived when the more fundamental understanding of truth is hermeneutically uncovered. However, a patient amount of recovery and retrieval is necessary before the clutter of theoretical modernity has been swept to one side.

It is not immediately obviously why Gadamer starts in this way but *Truth and Method* opens with a detailed analysis of modern aesthetic theory and its shortcomings. The exposition of *Truth and Method* in this chapter will start with historical understanding as an experience of the tradition (*TM*, Part 2).[4] Consideration of Gadamer's attitude to language as a pathway to truth will be dealt with in Chapter 5, 'Language and linguisticality', and his treatment of art and the aesthetic as aspects of truthfulness are considered in Chapter 6, 'Gadamer's aesthetics'.

TRUTH AS EXPERIENCE

Before discussing historical understanding as a dimension of truth Gadamer outlines the various ways the nature of experience can be conceived. This is important as a necessary preamble to his treatment of the different aspects of truth. Gadamer's treatment of truth commences from the thought that it cannot be captured within a theoretical framework. It cannot be something we can observe from a detached distance or in an objective way and claim to be 'scientific'. Truth, if it is anything, is to be participated in or encountered: something experienced. Experience is one of those slippery words and in philosophy we would be well advised to tread carefully round it. Gadamer, in discussing experience, alerts us to the many senses the term possesses.[5]

In empiricist philosophy it has many resonances, principally to do with the foundations of knowledge. Empiricism affirms that experiential knowledge is grounded if it is repeatable. For empiricism experience is fundamentally repetition, an endless recycling of the same. For instance one can speak of the sun rising tomorrow on the basis of the experience of its rising in the past in an almost endless sequence of repeated occurrences. The idea of experience as repetition is legitimate and has come to be part of the structure of inductive knowledge but repetition only captures one limited sense and ignores other possible nuances of meaning.

There is another way of speaking about experience, which actually pulls in the opposite direction to repetition. Instead of emphasizing the repeatable it draws attention to the qualities of the non-repeatable and the unique. Take, for instance, the phrase referring to something out of the ordinary: 'Last night I did something I have never done before, it was a real experience.' The essential character of the experience was its uniqueness, its unrepeatability. This kind of experience (*Erfahrung* as opposed to *Erlebnis*) is what Gadamer terms 'hermeneutic experience'. In genuine hermeneutic encounters one is surprised, pulled up short, in novel and unique ways. Expectations are thwarted as the taken-for-granted-ness of the everyday pattern confronts the unforeseen. Truth, as Gadamer describes it, is of the hermeneutic variety with this capacity to surprise and thwart expectations rather than to passively confirm them. Truth is revelation, what is opened up in the encounter between the familiar and the unfamiliar.

The sense in which genuine experience is hermeneutic is as follows. The constant irresolvable motion between part and whole has already been noted as a key feature of interpretation. In early hermeneutics this disjunction between part and whole was a tension in the understanding of texts, to be reduced by 'correct' interpretation. For Gadamer, the experience of truth is hermeneutical in that just as the part modifies the whole so the experience of truth encountered in the new, the novel, the unexpected, is in tension with the already understood. It is in the desire to assimilate or understand the novel in the light of the already experienced that truth takes on this hermeneutic dimension. There is a sense of the already understood and the alien, the different, the other, that in tandem with the already encountered constitutes hermeneutical truth for Gadamer. Once again, the analogy with reading is an appropriate one. Often one has the experience of being surprised by an appropriate expression, or a new way of expressing old truths. This experience of being pulled up short, the sense of 'I've never looked at it this way before', seems to be what Gadamer has in mind. No matter how many times a poem or novel are read they always manage to open up new lines of enquiry, new possibilities. The written text does not change but the interpretive possibilities, that is, for Gadamer, the truth possibilities, do, as they are endless. Gadamer models his idea of truth on Heidegger's notion of truth as disclosure, what is opened up and brought to light rather than the relationship of correspondence which is seen as a wrong turn in the Platonic notion of *aletheia* as adequation setting in train the whole history of a one-sided interpretation of the term.

Truth as the accumulation of scientific facts and propositions, the dream of the Enlightenment *philosophes*, with the *Encyclopaedia* as the totality of human wisdom between the covers of a book, is an impossibility since it ignores the contribution to truth made by the enquirer. Truth is experience. But what is it that is experienced? Doesn't experience make its possessor wiser? No. Experience, if it teaches anything, teaches its own limitations. The Enlightenment version of experience as the accumulation of knowledge is wildly optimistic and arrogant about the almost endless possibilities of human knowledge. Experience on the Enlightenment account is essentially incremental as it was for Hegel's dialectical movement from negation to its overcoming and ultimately complete supercession in the triumphant victory of spirit in the onward march of history. For Gadamer, the best that can be hoped for with experience is not knowledge but insight, insight into the fallibility of human possibilities and their essential limitations. Experience is no more than 'experience of human finitude' (*TM*, p. 357). Life is short and cannot be controlled however advanced science and technology takes itself to be. However safe we feel in a world of our own construction the sheer uncontrollability of things is a stark fact. The Greeks knew this well and Gadamer has in mind Aeschylus when he says the following:

> What a man has to learn through suffering is not this or that particular thing, but insight into the limitations of humanity, into the absoluteness of the barrier that separates man from the divine. It is ultimately a religious insight – the kind of insight that gave birth to Greek tragedy. (*TM*, p. 357).

Experience and insight are part of genuine wisdom and it is this that we have lost sight of in the modern world where we are more inclined to speak of the accumulation of knowledge in a so-called 'knowledge' society. Knowledge, with its ring of progress and modernity, forgets the dark side of human life. Life is short and we will never fully comprehend it. The truly wise person comes to an acknowledgement of this situation not in experience viewed as the accumulation of knowledge, for

> The experienced person proves to be . . . someone who is radically undogmatic; who, because of the many experiences he has had

and the knowledge he has drawn from them, is particularly well equipped to have new experiences and learn from them. The dialectic of experience has its proper fulfilment not in definitive knowledge but in the openness to experience that is made possible by experience itself.[6]

Experience, for Gadamer, is the quality of the undogmatic person open to new possibilities. And this ties in with Heidegger's vision of truth as another kind of openness, the one that brings itself out of concealment. So Gadamer, using Heidegger's notion of the fore-structure of understanding, rejects the modernist idea that truth is the accumulation of experience under the control of method. He replaces this with an account of truth as openness to experience. Experience is really a form of understanding. But understanding does not give rise to detached knowledge of this and that; it is principally self-understanding, an understanding of the self and for the self. The notion of the self is problematic in Gadamer, but whatever we take it to be it is not the Cartesian thinking I, it is a fragment of tradition hermeneutically related to the totality.

TRUTH IS HISTORICAL

Analytic philosophy is generally hostile to the idea that truth is historical and yet it is a position readily accepted by Gadamer. Truth is truth, say the analysts, and if a proposition, for example, is self-evidently the case it cannot be tainted by temporality or the passage of time. Anything that changes with time cannot be true because truth is timeless and changeless, it is sometimes argued. There is a long history, stretching back to the Greeks, to support this position but hermeneutics contests this point of view. Gadamer sums up his position as follows:

> History does not belong to us; we belong to it. Long before we understand ourselves through the process of self-examination, we understand ourselves in a self-evident way in the family, society, and state in which we live. The focus of subjectivity is a distorting mirror. The self-awareness of the individual is only a flickering in the closed circuits of historical life. *That is why the prejudices of the individual, far more than his judgements, constitute the historical reality of his being.*[7]

Modernity has placed too great an emphasis upon the sovereignty of the lone individual as the source of knowledge and insight, the legacy of Descartes and Kant no doubt.

Even before individuals seek to understand themselves as subjectivities they need to appreciate themselves as socially and culturally ascribed and constructed identities. And these identities reach back to a past to which they are intimately connected. But what is the nature of the connection? Gadamer speaks poetically of the 'closed circuits of historical life'. Are those who are attached to history helpless victims of the past, are they stuck within a history that is not only not of their own making but something from which they can never escape? Gadamer's suggestion is that although we cannot escape the co-ordinates of 'historical life' we are not the puppets of history pulled down by inherited prejudice. If we see prejudice as the condition of judgement some measure of self-awareness is possible when prejudices are confronted with the new and the unexpected. Of course, it is not possible to get a completely unclouded perspective on our own prejudice because, as has already been noted, prejudices are part of the way we understand, they are the pre-judgements that precede judgement. The 'flickering' suggests at least moments of self-understanding, insight and illumination, but nothing like the kind of transparent control over ourselves and the past often taken for granted when selves are referred to as transcendental egos or autonomous subjects. The key to understanding this passage is the concluding italicized sentence, '*That is why the prejudices of the individual, far more than his judgements, constitute the historical reality of his being*'. Individual judgements necessarily take place within a context of prejudice, this much we have already encountered. The sense of self, revealed in the quest for self-understanding, always takes place within the context of historical reality. Despite the post-Enlightenment image of selves as autonomous, self-reflective and unconstrained from the ties of social conformity, individuals are, on the contrary, rooted, embedded within a specific cultural milieu, within which movements towards self-understanding must always be reconciled. This specific milieu Gadamer calls tradition. Once again, opposing the received wisdom of modernity, Gadamer takes tradition to be, like prejudice, part of the background to our engagement with the world. It can never be made an object of investigation as we are always within it and can never find a point outside it to test its validity. In order to bring together tradition and historical life

(historicality), and in order to show how we are inescapably historical and part of tradition but not trapped and ensnared by it, attention can turn to a key term in Gadamer's lexicon, the 'horizon' and
what he terms the 'fusion of horizons'.

THE 'FUSION OF HORIZONS' AND THE PROBLEMS OF UNDERSTANDING THE PAST FROM THE SITE OF THE PRESENT

The term horizon, occurring as it does in the work of Nietzsche and
Husserl, is not original. In the hands of Gadamer it operates something like Humboldt's idea that language provides the speaker with
not just a means of communication but a standpoint from which to
view the world, a world-view. As one acquires the capacity to use language, and as a result of the process of acculturation, one at the same
time acquires a 'horizon', a perspective on the world. The term is
particularly appropriate because it suggests a panoramic vista from
a particular perspective. As Gadamer says, 'The concept of the
"horizon" suggests itself because it expresses the superior breadth
of vision that the person who is trying to understand must have'
(*TM*, p. 305). The thought here is that to have a horizon is to have a
perspective upon the world. This is in part acquired via language;
hence the horizon is linguistical in a very basic sense.[8] Language provides the horizon as both disclosure and limit. To be discovered later
is the fact that the 'fusion of horizons' is ultimately an aspiration; it
never can be fully achieved or finally completed. The suggestion that
an easy accommodation of one horizon by the other with settled
harmony and complete agreement ensuing is very far from Gadamer's
intention. Yet despite never achieving total transparency of understanding with the other the need for interpretation is constant and
ever present. Gadamer confirms this when he offers the following, 'the
fusion of the horizons of interpretation is nothing that one ever
reaches' because 'the horizon of interpretation changes constantly,
just as our visual horizon also varies with every step that we take'.[9]

The horizon is not fixed; it is constantly changing and modified
little by little over time. Not by the sheer weight of accumulated
experience but by a process of expansion. A 'fusion of horizons'
embodies a measure of agreement and this in turn is a partial understanding: '*Understanding is always the fusion of . . . horizons*'
(*TM*, p. 306). The thought here is that a horizon can be brought into
contact with another horizon. Instead of one obliterating the other

a process of fusion takes place. And Gadamer's idea is that this happens both down and across time, diachronically and synchronically. There are many ways to cash in the metaphor of the *fusion* but the most obvious relates to understanding the past (although it includes interpersonal and even inter-cultural understanding).

Is the past a foreign country, even the past of our own language and culture? Sure enough things are done differently there but is it a remote and alien place? And how are those in the present connected to the past? If horizons are in the present how do we connect to horizons in the past? These are some of the unsettling questions Gadamer raises when he evokes the image of the fusion of horizons.

Relativism, the view that there are no objective standards and every perspective is ultimately self-referential, denies the possibility of bridging historical distances: more than time often divides epochs. There are the conceptual difficulties of linguistic and cultural changes making words in the present alien and incomprehensible to those in the past. There are a multitude of problems surrounding the gap between the present and the past at all sorts of levels. Take for instance the hermeneutic problem of understanding ancient texts. Aristotle's world is far removed from the present. An ancient term like *eudaimonia*, for convenience sake often translated as 'happiness' and yet quite unlike a modern idea of satisfaction or being contented with one's lot, is just one example of the problem of historical distance. What chances do we have of correctly interpreting Aristotle's texts and seeking to penetrate the lost civilization of ancient Greece with its manifold practices, beliefs, customs, remote from the modern world? Can we correctly interpret the past? It would be a mistaken assumption to refine an interpretive method in such a way that the interpreting subject hits upon the correct interpretation. This would be to repeat the mistakes Gadamer exposed in the scientific method; to transpose this method to interpretation of the past would be mistaken. However, if were to regard the past as possessing its own horizon and the task of comprehension for the interpreter in the present is to engage with the 'lost' horizon then another possibility emerges.

Understanding is not a question of an active subject casting a meaning on an inert and dead object; on the contrary, both the present and the past have horizons that may be productively brought together. The event of understanding is a negotiation of the present and the past; this is invariably linguistic or via an artefact (effectively a language substitute since it stands in need of interpretation). To speak of an ancient text possessing a horizon is to speak of a world-view. The world-view of the past makes a claim, via text, on the present. The ancient text for all its outdatedness and antiquity still speaks in its presentation of its horizon. The idea of the fusion of horizons, in some ways explains the nature, and justifies the existence, of the philosophical and literary canon. Why do countless generations keep turning back to Plato and Aristotle, Aeschylus and Shakespeare? It is because these texts still have something to say to those in the present. They seek to draw the present into their respective horizons; they seek to draw us into dialogue and they seek to communicate their truths.

But Gadamer is not merely accounting for the possibility of translation and interpretation of ancient texts using established hermeneutical principles; he is providing a model for all understanding. What he also manages to establish is that the dislocated subjectivity is a myth. All understanding takes place from within an embedded horizon but that horizon is necessarily and ubiquitously interconnected with the past. It would be a mistake to say we are always locked into the past but we are ceaselessly in a present through which the past speaks. This is the character of tradition itself being made up of past, present and future. Our attempts at self-understanding have a futural element (we are always projecting into the unknown future) but our understandings in the present constantly draw upon, fuse with, the past. The language through which we articulate the present resonates with the meanings from the past and they continue to be operative in the present; this gives a sense of what Gadamer means by 'effective historical consciousness'.

EFFECTIVE HISTORICAL CONSCIOUSNESS

Gadamer refers to 'effective history', meaning the history of effects: '*understanding is, essentially, a historically effected event*' (*TM*, p. 300). This is a difficult thought to grasp. What Gadamer has in mind is that the position of the interpreter, or the one who seeks to understand, is not fixed (as science conceives its detached observer to be); on the contrary, the interpreter is always, as part of tradition, the effect of prior interpretation. There can be no neutral position from which interrogation or understanding takes place as the site of interpretation is itself the effect of the past upon the present. The sovereignty of the subject is once again taken to be fictional since the interpreter is little more than the effect of tradition rather than its controlling subject. What then is one conscious of in 'effective historical consciousness'? We are conscious of the tradition and the way it has its effect. The prejudices of the individual can never be raised to the level of consciousness; this we have already established. Because the prejudices are themselves the condition of consciousness they can never be raised to the level of reflective judgement. But the effect of the disruption of the prejudices can be experienced, felt as an effect, that is. Once again, the model of textual interpretation will provide the clue to unravelling the identity between understanding and interpretation. When reading a text it is understood not simply by making sense of the words on the page but by permitting the horizon of the text to fuse with the horizon of the reader in such a way that the reader is affected by the encounter with the text. It is a common enough experience to be disrupted by the effect a text can have on the reader; often what we take for granted can be redefined, changed and realigned by the act of reading. Gadamer speaks here of consciousness. A consciousness in the act of reading is never fully present to itself *but* it can be made aware of changes taking place (in that consciousness) as the text has an effect. In its capacity to surprise, delight, intrigue, confuse, and so on, we can speak of the effect the text has upon consciousness. Gadamer seeks to dispel the orthodox idea that consciousness is reflection fully in control of itself: he conceives of consciousness as both active and re-active.

The idea of an effect is important in another way. Not only is the reader an effect of the text, as the horizons of reader and text fuse, but the reader is also revealed to be part of an historical effect: 'Every encounter with tradition that takes place within historical consciousness involves the experience of a tension between the text and the present' (*TM*, p. 306).

There is a constant dialogue at work in interpretation, a dialogue between the past and the present. The past does not have to be the distant past of antiquity; it can be the recent past of a moment just gone. The point is that in both cases the same hermeneutical problem arises: how can the interpreter in the present accommodate or negotiate meanings external to current consciousness? Gadamer's whole point is that there are no meanings external to current consciousness since meaning itself is always produced by the coming together of the immediate and the point of tradition one seeks to understand.

DIALOGUE

This takes us to the next crucial move in Gadamer's argument, namely, that understanding is always part of a dialogue, hence, is dialogical in nature. The character of the dialogue has already been suggested in the fusion of horizons because when horizons interface they engage in dialogue. Or at least this is Gadamer's vision. Some may see the coming together of horizons or consciousnesses as the opportunity for gladiatorial combat. They may see the object of the encounter to be the supercession or the obliteration of the Other, whereas for Gadamer understanding is the accommodation of the Other. This was what was meant by the fusion of horizons; the point is not to overshadow and abolish the horizon of the past (conceived as other), but to show how that horizon has been taken up and expanded in the present. This is a question of not exposing the weaknesses of the past such that they had to be superseded by the present but by bringing out the sense in which the present is just the past in a new form.

Gadamer illustrates his hermeneutics of dialogue by highlighting two aspects from the history of philosophy. His first concerns a radical re-reading of early Socratic dialogue.[10] In these early dialogues Socrates is witnessed doing battle with the leading sophists of the day. Using the tricks of sophistry as much as his opponents he succeeds in silencing many of his interlocutors. The orthodox view of these early Platonic works is that Socrates paradoxically reveals the fragility of truth and knowledge by exposing the limitations of sophistry. He does this by defending a version of absolute truth against the dangerous relativistic sophistry of his opponents. Socrates does argumentative battle with his adversaries and through the force of hardnosed logic exposes the limitations of weak argument.

Socrates, according to the standard reading, epitomizes the triumph of logic over bogus reasoning. Against this heroic account Gadamer offers another picture. Socrates speaks of himself as a midwife and this self-description fits in well with the Gadamerian interpretation. As midwife Socrates is not in possession of truth but is there at its birth. Like a midwife he is not the central figure but a facilitator. The real birth of truth is what happens in *genuine* dialogue. After all, the early Platonic texts are not treatises but conversations, everyday exchanges, dialogues in the most informal sense. Not only does Socrates facilitate truth he facilitates dialogue. Socrates, as the purveyor of Aunt Sally arguments he sets up merely to knock down, and Socrates as the exposer of sham wisdom, pretension and arrogance in his opponents in argument, gives way to an alternative interpretation. Here Socrates is only one voice in a larger conversation where all are participants rather than disputants; he provides the conditions for the emergence of truth from the collective voice of the conversation. Truth, whatever it is, can only emerge from dialogue (essentially a conversation with and within tradition). For this reason, the early works of Plato are written in dialogical form, not just because this makes for a stylish and dramatic literary presentation. The works are in dialogue form because truth *is* dialogue.

There are many things to be said of dialogue that are equally appropriate to truth. One essential aspect is incompleteness. A genuine dialogue or conversation is characterized by its very lack of completeness and structure. We speak of 'falling into' or 'striking up' conversations suggesting that they are never planned and just happen. No one knows where they will lead as they are not regulated by rules and conventions and yet they have a kind of structure of their own. Gadamer comments: 'What emerges [in a dialogue] is neither mine nor yours and hence so far transcends the interlocutors' subjective opinions that even the person leading the conversation knows that he does not know' (*TM*, p. 368). He adds that: 'We say that we "conduct" a conversation, but the more genuine a conversation is, the less its conduct lies within the will of either partners. Thus a genuine conversation is never the one that we wanted to conduct' (*TM*, p. 383). Dialogues move in unpredictable directions, unaccountably changing in tone from frivolous to the deeply serious, often leading from something as innocent as a chance remark. And the authentic dialogue reveals something about its participants. Dialogue is the very opposite of self-reflexive, monadic, introspective thought. It is intrinsically spoken (as opposed to written or merely thought) and it takes place in a public forum. All of these qualities of the dialogue are equally applicable to Gadamer's conception of truth (and his conception of Plato's conception of truth). In the genuine dialogue the participants change as initial assumptions are challenged, modified, held up to scrutiny in the public court of appeal, in the dialogue itself. It was suggested that the prejudices sustaining understanding could never be made the object of scrutiny. This can be taken as read but prejudices can rise to the fore in dialogue as they are frequently challenged and surprised in dialogical encounters. This is not a case of raising prejudice to the level of self-consciousness, more a matter of becoming aware of fundamental reference points by having them challenged or taken by surprise. This is not so surprising. A productive dialogue often has the effect of forcing one to see things differently and in a new light.

THE LOGIC OF QUESTION AND ANSWER

Another seminal point in the history of philosophy Gadamer focuses upon to emphasize the importance of dialogue is taken from the work of the British philosopher and historian R. G. Collingwood. Collingwood, a lone voice in Oxford philosophy in the 1930s, defended a version of historicism completely at odds with the anti-historical 'realism' of his colleagues. This realism, to which Collingwood took such a strong objection, postulated the idea of a timeless truth and took all philosophical texts as successful or failed in relation to their capacity to demonstrate logically invincible argument. Collingwood, as a practising archaeologist and historian, used to the interpretive element within historical understanding, took an opposing view. He devised the term the 'logic of question and answer' to combat the position of his opponents that philosophical texts should be judged according to the lights of a universally valid logic. He opposed this with an alternative logic of dialogue where all philosophical texts are taken to be tentative responses to previously formulated questions in earlier texts. The realists thought it possible, it seems, to work line by line through the whole of a philosophical text and establishing its meaning in terms of its logical coherence and little else. A text could be surveyed to assess whether the arguments it constructs are valid or invalid. Collingwood rejects such a procedure as no more than logic chopping. Its fundamental mistake is to neglect the essentially historical nature of past texts. On the other hand, he favours regarding a philosophical text as a response to a question or series of questions. So, for example, instead of looking at the logic of the arguments enshrined in the *Meditations* it would be more appropriate to ask what Descartes was attempting to achieve, what problems had he set himself, what problems had he inherited from his philosophical predecessors and how do we seek to approach and solve them? These questions provide the vital context for interpreting Descartes for they reveal something about the text that a mere inspection of the logic of Descartes's formal arguments ignores.

According to Collingwood, his approach to philosophical texts would yield up more interesting and historically 'accurate' accounts. Not only would it make the *context* in which a work was written as important as the text itself, it would reveal something else essential to Gadamer's hermeneutics. Collingwood failed to stress this but implicitly he bore testament to the fact that all understanding is essentially dialogical. The attempt to understand a work in the history of philosophy is a metaphor for understanding itself. Textual interpretation involves getting into a dialogue with the text and Collingwood realized this point.

In Collingwood's celebrated autobiography[11] he accounts for the origins of his logic of question and answer in the following anecdote. In gazing upon the Albert Memorial in London one day he suspended his own subjective response to the monument – he found it ugly and unpleasant – and sought to penetrate beyond his own reaction. In its place he thought alternatively in terms of the architect as producer of the object, and what he had in mind when creating the monument. What was it he had in mind when he created the piece? To establish this, it was not necessary (or possible) to penetrate the mind of the architect. But interpretation necessitated establishing the range of possibilities open to him. This is a historical question and the details of the nature of the commission, the parameters within which the architect was required to work, were all pertinent questions in the quest to make sense of the monument.

What hit Collingwood with such force was the requirement for *re-enactment* and *retrieval* as part of the process of historical understanding. To understand the meaning of the Albert Memorial it was vital to regard it as an answer to a question or series of questions. When looked at in this light, that is in the light of the historical context in which it was created, its meaning became more coherent. Collingwood transposes his newfound thoughts on the meaning of the Albert Memorial to the question of understanding texts in the history of philosophy.

The meaning of Plato's *Republic* is to be established in terms of the questions Plato sought to address in his text and this involves a good deal of retrieval of the historical context surrounding the production of the work. The role of the historian of philosophy is, to the best of his or her ability, to retrieve those questions. A text has a broad meaning in excess of the literal words of which it is composed. It always goes beyond itself. The historian of philosophy needs to capture this excess of meaning in his/her interpretation of the text and the logic of question and answer is designed to open up lines of enquiry to facilitate the comprehension of the excess.

A frequent mistake, making for bad history of philosophy, is to impose contemporary categories upon an ancient work. In the case of Plato, a grave injustice to the work is done if one sees it exclusively through the lens of modern political ideologies. The trend in the 1930s and 1940s to view the *Republic* as an ancient precursor to totalitarian thought prevents an understanding of the text in its own terms and imposes upon the text a range of meanings quite alien to the text itself. In Gadamerian terms, to impose exclusively contemporary categories upon an ancient work is to effectively silence the text, to refuse to engage it in dialogue.

This is the point at which Gadamer is critical of Collingwood. Although he acknowledges the importance of Collingwood he criticizes his logic of question and answer for failing to acknowledge the historicity of the historian. Although Collingwood acknowledges the importance of retrieving the ancient text from contemporary deformations, he fails to realize that the interpreter is also an effect of tradition and history and never interprets from a fixed point. The questions one asks of a text are always a result of the tradition and hence the questions keep changing as one reads into a work, wittingly or unwittingly, one's own questions. The problem with this approach for all its methodological guidance is a failure to account for the historicity of the interpreter. The backward movement towards the question of the text neglects the fact that the interpretation of the text's question is always, problematically, from the point of view, of the horizon, of the interpreter in the present. Whereas for Collingwood it is always possible to use the logic of question and answer to achieve fidelity in retrieving and unearthing the original meaning of the historical text for Gadamer the meaning of the text is constantly changing; interpretation and re-interpretation are ceaseless tasks. The logic of question and answer could be taken a stage further – by showing how the questions and the answers are ceaselessly being re-defined in the process of interpretation. Making sense of an ancient text is a question of engaging in dialogue with it. The horizon of the text opens up questions to the interpreter and the interpreter in turn defines questions in relation to what is opened up in the dialogue.

Collingwood exposes the limitations of an over literal and purely logical approach to the reading of historical texts. The logic of question and answer is a useful guide to interpreting texts in the history of philosophy but its significance is wider as it gives access to a vital hermeneutical principle, which is that language always goes beyond itself. Gadamer says:

> A person who wants to understand must question what lies behind what is said. He must understand it as an answer to a question. If we go back *behind* what is said, then we inevitably ask questions *beyond* what is said. We understand the sense of the text only by acquiring the horizon of the question . . . (*TM*, p. 370)

NOTES

1 Brice Wachterhauser has termed Gadamer's account of truth 'perspectival realism'. See Wachterhauser (1994).
2 According to Heidegger the Greek word *aletheia*, although it comes to mean truth (in the sense of correspondence) literally means (truth as) 'unconcealment', bringing something out of darkness and into the light. See Heidegger's essay 'On the essence of truth' in *Martin Heidegger: Basic Writings* (Krell, 1978).
3 Part 1 is entitled, 'The question of truth as it emerges in the experience of art'; Part 2, 'The extension of the question of truth to understanding in the human sciences'; and Part 3, 'The ontological shift of hermeneutics guided by language'.
4 Entitled 'The extension of the question of truth to understanding in the human sciences'.
5 In passing, it is worth recording that Gadamer's training as both a philosopher and a philologist (one trained in the art of philology, 'the science of language, especially in its historical and comparative aspects' (*Concise Oxford Dictionary*)) illustrates something of a common concern with analytic philosophy's discussion of questions via the language used to formulate those questions.
6 *TM*, p. 355.
7 *TM*, pp. 276–7.
8 The power of language to enable one to 'see' and to 'see differently' is alluded to in the idea of the horizon. It is also an important motif in the later work of Ludwig Wittgenstein, especially in the part on 'seeing aspects' in Section xi of *Philosophical Investigations* (Wittgenstein, 2001).
9 Gadamer (2004), p. 61.
10 See *TM*, 'The model of Platonic dialectic', pp. 362–9.
11 Collingwood (1982).

CHAPTER 5

GADAMER ON LANGUAGE AND LINGUISTICALITY

To experience a place within history, that is, within tradition, is one way of encountering truth. Gadamer mentions two others, these being language and art. We will consider art in the next chapter; in this chapter the focus is upon Gadamer's treatment of language. The chapter presents an assessment of language and its importance for philosophical hermeneutics as it is dealt with in *Truth and Method*[1] and the later works. Much has been made of the so-called 'linguistic turn' in twentieth-century analytic philosophy; in like fashion the importance of language in Gadamer cannot be overstated. However, this is hardly a linguistic turn: the centrality of language is at the heart of the philosophical traditions within which Gadamer works.

PHILOSOPHY AND LANGUAGE

Since the birth of philosophy in classical antiquity there has been an appreciation of the intimate connection between language and philosophy. However, because language was often taken to be the vehicle of thought, assuming cognition to be superior to the language expressing it, thinking overshadowed language. Language was taken to be a transparent medium through which thoughts travelled. To use a metaphor, it is as though thought was the message and language the telephone wire along which it travelled. The fundamental project of philosophy since ancient times was to appreciate the centrality of thinking; after all it was thought that represented our highest achievement, and there was nothing higher than human cognition save divine thought. Thought had this revered status not only because, as Aristotle states, it is the most divine part of us, but also because rational thought gives access to an accurate picture of the world via language. Most theories of linguistic meaning are *designative* in origin. Such a theory states that language is meaningful because it pictures, represents or designates the world. On this theory the word 'chair' is meaningful because there are objects in the world called chairs for which the word stands. And language is meaningful because we can accurately represent the world by using words to talk about objects. More than this, words represent states of mind and thus accurately articulate and communicate descriptions of mental states, moods, emotions and feelings. Put simply, we can represent the way the world is to ourselves, both mentally and physically, and we can communicate with each other because language is at its most basic a system of signs standing proxy for real objects.

There is a venerable tradition in philosophy subscribing to this basic article of faith about the power of language to depict and designate. It starts with Plato and Aristotle and re-emerges with modern versions of empiricism and rationalism. The empiricists, like the English philosopher John Locke (following Thomas Hobbes), speak of words having significance because they stand for the private sensations of the speaker.[2] And in more recent times the early linguistic analysis of Bertrand Russell and Ludwig Wittgenstein subscribes to more sophisticated versions of designation. Wittgenstein's *Tractatus Logico-Philosophicus*, a classic modern text in this tradition, advances the picture theory where meaningful language is taken to picture reality (or rather possible states of affairs).

The designative theory regards words as representatives of things or objects. Following from this it takes sentences to offer unambiguous and incontrovertible statements about the world itself (that is, beyond language). Philosophers subscribing to this position generally refer to these sentences as propositions; propositions being indicative sentences asserting or denying something about the way the world is. They are statements about what is the case and the task of linguistic philosophy is to test their logical validity both in their own terms and in terms of their relations to other propositions. Basically a proposition is a unit of sense coming between perceptions and states of affairs. Although technical and advanced versions of designation dominate theories of language in Anglo-American philosophy it is not the only way philosophers and others have conceived language. Another major position in the tradition is sometimes referred to as the expressivist view of language.[3] Here language's capacity to represent the world is subordinated to the power of words to express something concerning what it is to be human. And this is made possible by the fact that language at bottom is sustained and authenticated not by designation but by various forms of linguistic solidarity. An implicit and explicit network of agreements regulating meaning and language use sustains language and it is the rules deriving from a large measure of social and linguistic convention and consensus that expressive theories emphasize. Language is fundamentally a social, cultural and historical phenomenon and any detailed study should start from an appreciation of this vital fact.

Expressivism has a long history but in the modern period it really starts with the German philosopher Johann Georg Hamann (1730–88).[4] This tradition continues with Herder and Humboldt and extends to Heidegger and Gadamer. The hermeneutical attitude to language is fundamentally expressivist. This is a radical alternative to designation, a position taken up and explored by Wittgenstein, for example, in his later work. When Wittgenstein speaks of the meaning of a word being its use – rather than its referent – he exemplifies the expressivist position.[5] Here a word is meaningful not because a word stands for an object but because its meaning, and the ways it can be used in sentences (and the ways it fits 'performatively' into the fabric of everyday life), is sanctioned by consensus, agreement and convention. The expressivist position moves away from the idea of taking language to be a representational grid upon the world, and embraces something more akin to a system of ciphers, sustained by rules of use. The meaning of a word is defined by the conventional regularities of usage; the thought that language is sustained by its anchorage in what it represents is an illusion. The source of linguistic meaning is the central distinction between the expressivist and the designative positions. There are other significant differences and these stem from this fundamental difference. As the name implies expressivism concerns the power of language to express, specifically the power to express what it is to be human.

In an example given by the Canadian philosopher Charles Taylor,[6] a person entering a railway carriage with the announcement, 'Phew, it's hot in here!' is not seeking to use language to describe a state of affairs or communicate to the others in the carriage something they had failed to realize. Here is a paradigm of language used in an expressive way. The declamation says more than it says; the subtext presumes a common world. Although the experience in the railway carriage is one of mild discomfort it is a world in common and the utterance says more about what is shared than the temperature of the carriage. Language here both draws on a given solidarity – we would not understand each other if it did not – and makes explicit solidarity: we are all in this together. A simple and trivial example, no doubt, but it makes explicit the obvious point that language does far more than describe a world. In much modern philosophy words are likened to tools; this is a helpful image as it takes language to be something practical and part of our involvement with the world rather than a detached description of that world. Wittgenstein's 'language-games' and J. L. Austin's 'performative' utterance, where language is part of a performance rather than a description of it, bring out the tool-like quality of language. To think of language as a tool is to take up a non-designative position. We might say for the expressivist language actually constitutes the world: the human world is made possible by the intimate solidarities of language and cultural life and without these solidarities there would be no human world. This sentiment is echoed in Gadamer's distinction between 'world' and 'environment'. 'The concept of *world* is . . . opposed to the concept of *environment*, which all living beings in the world possess' (*TM*, p. 443). What distinguishes world from environment is language,

> [W]hich is not just one of man's possessions in the world; rather on it depends the fact that man has a *world* at all. The world as world exists for man as for no other creature that is in the world. But this world is verbal in nature. (*TM*, p. 443)

This is not say the world is made up of words; it means that our world is made possible by language. And because language is a product, or a condition of, social life, our world is quintessentially social. Whether a measure of social organization ushers in language or social organization is the precondition for language is a moot point. Rousseau and others discuss it, in the search for the origins of language, so common in the eighteenth century.

Attention was drawn earlier to the power of language to express what it is to be human. We normally think of literature, poetry and drama as the most potent expressions of human achievement. Designation tends to ignore these expressive uses of language as somehow secondary or less important than the unembellished language of formal propositions. This whole distinction, between the metaphorical and the literal, is readily challenged. Is not literary, poetic language as powerful and world disclosing as those sentences that putatively describe the world? One of the strengths of the expressivist position is its refusal to divide language up into the literal and the figurative. All living language, the language of everyday conversation, the language of poetry, even the language of propositions, have expression as a common denominator.

GADAMER'S ACCOUNT OF THE NATURE OF LANGUAGE

We have already identified Gadamer as part of the expressivist tradition in so far as it emerges from the hermeneutical tradition. We can look at the various positions Gadamer subscribes to, all of them consistent with versions of expressivist approaches to language. The cardinal mistake of representational accounts of language is the assumption that because there is a gap between words and that which they represent, a language can be examined with scientific accuracy for it is assumed that the power of representation can be assessed with precision and detachment. Gadamer's rejection of this position starts from the simple fact that we are always already involved with language and cannot make it an object of investigation. The expression, used by Heidegger and Gadamer, derived from the German romantic poet Hölderlin, is that 'we are a conversation',[7] suggesting we are thoroughly bound and bound up with language. As well as affirming what we have already noted, namely that the conversation plays an important part for Gadamer, it also denies the possibility of extricating ourselves from language. There can be no point outside language from which to test it; we are thoroughly immersed in linguisticality. Further, there can be no philosophy or science of language that gets to the heart of what language is. Philosophical hermeneutics does not offer a philosophy of language because such a theoretically based activity, as traditionally understood, is precisely an attempt to understand the power of language and the relationship between language and the world in a quasi-scientific, theoretical, fashion. To understand the phenomenon of language, for Gadamer, is to seek to discover what language *is*, its being, even though there can be no stepping outside of it. The earlier examination of experience implicitly concludes that every aspect of life has a hermeneutical structure and that structure is ultimately linguistical. All experience is revealed as something that can only be expressed via language for it too has the hermeneutical structure of language.

THE HERMENEUTICS OF THE SPOKEN WORD

There is an orthodox view in the history of Western philosophy, only recently subjected to criticism in the work of Jacques Derrida[8] and elsewhere, that the spoken word has authority over its written counterpart. This by virtue of the fact that historically, it is assumed, speech preceded writing but the ordering also has a philosophical justification. This prioritizing of speech over writing is as old as Socrates. The dangers of writing are a constant theme in the dialogues of Plato and account for the fact that Socrates never wrote. The real fear is that words, once frozen in written form, will be misunderstood and misrepresented without the presence of the speaker to clear up ambiguities and unintended meanings. In live speech language is at its most authentic.

Gadamer regards the real task of his hermeneutics as revitalizing the written word in such a way that it returns to the condition of speech. This goes back to the idea of language as part of dialogue. The condition of language as dialogue is the real point of Gadamer's favouring of speech over writing. He is not taking up the familiar philosophical stance of finding in speech the authentic voice of a self-presencing subject. In speech, and thought is only internalized speech, we recognize Plato's soul in dialogue with itself (see *Sophist* (263e) and *Theaetetus* (189e)).

Gadamer refers to the written word as both alienated and in some sense inferior to writing. Of alienation he says, 'All writing is a kind of alienated speech, and its signs need to be transformed back into speech and meaning' (*TM*, p. 393). A similar thought is expressed when he comments:

> Thus written texts present the real hermeneutical task. Writing is self-alienation. Overcoming it, reading the text, is thus the highest task of understanding. Even the pure signs of an inscription can be seen properly and articulated correctly only if the text can be transformed back into language. (*TM*, pp. 390–1)

Later he says, 'in relation to language, writing seems a secondary phenomenon' (*TM*, p. 392), secondary, no doubt, to speech.

Only once we appreciate language as speech will we come to realize that language is essentially dialogue. In seeking to interpret a written text we can only understand it in the round if we can bring the dead words on the page to life; to do this we need to treat the text not as an inert repository of fixed meanings but as a partner, a partner in dialogue. And a dialogue is essentially spoken not written. The written word is somehow underscored by speech. Once again speech is not some hotline to the subjectivity of the speaker; it is the constant play of dialogue in which meanings are constantly under way being in the process of negotiation and re-negotiation. So to understand a written text we need to treat it as a partner in dialogue and seek to revitalize the written word, bring it to life by engaging it in conversation, which is all understanding is anyway. The process of revitalization takes us back to the themes we have already met with, those being dialogue and the question and answer of historical understanding. As meaning is dialogical the sense of a text for the reader/interpreter is provisional as it in time gives way to different interpretations.

'BEING THAT CAN BE UNDERSTOOD IS LANGUAGE'

'Being that can be understood is language',[9] Gadamer declares, echoing as it does Heidegger's famous 'Language is the house of being'. It sounds a completely superfluous question, but why do we use language at all? What is the point of language? This is a fundamental question and the obvious answer is, 'the point of language is to communicate'. This, from the perspective of hermeneutics, is very much a superficial response as it begs the deeper question what motivates us to communicate with each other in the first place? The idea that language is nothing other than the transmission and reception of nuggets of information reduces language to telegraphy and fails to take account of more fundamental issues. Without language there would be no world, this much we have already established, so language is about negotiating and making sense of a human world largely of our own construction. If we speak of *being* rather than the *world* we can say that the impulse to use language is part of the desire to interrogate and make sense of being. This essentially Heideggerian thought is where Gadamer's account of language begins. The real meaning of communicate is not, then, the transmission and reception of data and information; it is cognate with the Latin *'communicare'* with the suggestion of what is shared and what is held in common.

Towards the end of *Truth and Method*[10] Gadamer announces the following: 'Being that can be understood is language' – a slogan, no doubt, but a fairly ambiguous one. Language is the means by which we come to understand being is the most obvious reading. So in one sense the point of language is to enable us, as a group, as a community of language-users, to understand the nature of being: what being is and how we are related to it is always an issue for us. All language interrogates being, we might say. But it says more than this. Whatever we come to understand about being is always through the medium of language. This does not mean that all being is understandable through language; this kind of totalizing thought, reminiscent of old-fashioned 'hard science', is anathema to Gadamer's position. On the contrary, he is at pains to show how our understanding of the world is tentative, provisional, and never in a position to totally explain and understand being. 'Being that can be understood is language' means that whatever can be understood about being is necessarily linguistical. This is a radical and far-reaching insight. It suggests that all of our appropriations of being, in fact everything we do and are conscious of, is via language. Language is everywhere and completely dominates our view of the world. No doubt Gadamer would contest any view about understanding that presupposes something non-linguistic. For example we could speak of art and music as offering forms of understanding that make no reference to language, as they are to be understood either visually or musically. Expressions of pain can be spoken of as pre-linguistic having no linguistic and cognitive element to them. In the religious sphere we may refer to the mystical that is precisely that which leaves language behind and yet in some ways presents a form of understanding. These positions are untenable; what precisely is a form of understanding that cannot be put into words, and what exactly is it that one understands if it cannot be expressed in words? Gadamer's challenge is to produce an instance of understanding that cannot be communicated via language, and this is surely impossible. And the most philosophical aspect of Gadamer's position is, once again, the challenge to that most ubiquitous philosophical view, namely that thought itself gives rise to forms of understanding that need not be expressed via language because on this view it is thought itself that makes language possible.

If 'being that can be understood is language', does this mean that there are no parts of being that cannot be reached by language?

Also, does this mean that language is ultimately capable of expressing all that can be expressed about being within itself? Nothing could be further from the Gadamerian position. Language brings aspects of being to light, that is, it makes it comprehensible to human consciousness, but as even Heraclitus realized, being constantly outmanoeuvres our ability to express it. Being is always going to go beyond our ability to express it, not only because language is limited but also because being is both disclosed and concealed by language. An example of this phenomenon is revealed in an analysis of propositions. Even a proposition, as a statement about the world, contains both the *said* and the *unsaid*. The said is obviously what the proposition is about but the unsaid is what motivates it, what question to which the proposition itself is an answer. Every utterance is surrounded by this element of the unsaid. Returning briefly to Collingwood's 'logic of question and answer', we can justifiably regard the proposition as an answer to a prior question and thus this element of the unstated and the unsaid surrounds all statements and propositions. The hermeneutical task is to uncover and lay bare the unsaid by drawing it into an explicit dialogue with the said.

Gadamer has been accused of 'linguistic idealism', of making language an autonomous creation, some spiritual demiurge or power over and above the free choices of autonomous individuals. Gadamer freely consents to the Heideggerian formulation that we do not speak language but it is language that speaks us. On the face of it this is a bizarre and counter-intuitive claim given that we feel language, more than anything else, is something we have power over. What sense can it make to regard language as that which speaks rather than speakers?

Those who accuse Gadamer of linguistic idealism claim that he sees in language a power beyond human subjectivity; almost as if language is divine or at the very least, like the Hegelian *Geist* or Spirit, whose odyssey is the development of world history and individuals are merely the puppets of spirit. Gadamer does deny language is under the control of human subjectivity but this does not reduce individual language-users to ciphers of the great golem 'Language'. Gadamer's denial of human subjectivity as the controller of linguistic meaning is an anti-Cartesian move. He denies that it is the power of thought that guarantees linguistic meaning and goes on to show that it is a product of human dialogical interaction. No one knows how and why language changes; it is in one sense democratically beyond the grasp of wilful human subjectivities. Language constantly changes in the light of the endless dialogical exchanges within the context of tradition and history and these changes are beyond the control of individuals, linguistic groups and any agency seeking to control the movement of language. It is in this sense that it is fair to say that 'language speaks us'. The grammatical rules by which language is regulated, the burden of linguistic tradition, are all in place long before we, as individuals, enter the linguistic arena. Of course, hermeneutics demonstrates the sense in which we make language our own, even though we inherit a larger configuration, English or German, out of which our own voice within the larger configuration is forged.[11]

NOTES

1 The final third section of *Truth and Method*, 'The ontological shift of hermeneutics guided by language', is devoted to a consideration of the nature of language and its changing fortunes in the history of philosophy. Gadamer's argument here is, at times, quite difficult to follow. The central thrust of his position is spelt out when he claims, 'language is the universal medium in which understanding occurs' (*TM*, p. 389).

2 'Words in their primary or immediate signification stand for nothing but the ideas in the mind of him that uses them, how imperfectly soever or carelessly those ideas are collected form the things which they are supposed to represent' (from John Locke's *An Essay concerning Human Understanding* (1690), 3.2.1).

3 The terms 'designative' and 'expressive' are taken from Charles Taylor's essay 'Theories of Meaning' in Taylor (1985).

4 Hamman is best known as a contemporary critic of Immanuel Kant's critical philosophy but his work on language is important as it inaugurates a whole tradition of thinking about language which culminates in the work of Heidegger and Gadamer.

5 The proximity of Wittgenstein to Gadamer and his complex relationship to the expressivist position is the subject of my book *Wittgenstein and Gadamer: Towards a Post-Analytic Philosophy of Language* (Lawn, 2004). For some further consideration of the Gadamer–Wittgenstein relationship see Chapter 8.

6 See the essay 'Theories of Meaning' in Taylor (1985).

7 'Man has learned much since morning/For we are a conversation, and we can listen/To one another.' From Holderlin's poem 'Celebration of Peace'.

8 The priority of speech over writing is challenged in *Of Grammatology*.

9 *TM*, p. 474.

10 *TM*, p. 474.

11 Many critics have challenged the sense in which we find our own voice within language. Because of what Habermas terms 'systematically distorted communication', speakers fail to find a voice other than that which they inherit via the forces of ideology. The language we inherit, it can be argued against Gadamer, is always someone else's and is infected by the distortions of power, class and gender.

CHAPTER 6

GADAMER'S AESTHETICS

ART AND TRUTH

The exposition of *Truth and Method*, in earlier chapters, commenced with a rejection of conceptions of truth derived from philosophical method, hence Gadamer's title. We also noted that in place of truth as method Gadamer sought to return to a more fundamental encounter with truth; that is, truth as (hermeneutical) experience. The focus so far has been on the experiences of truth in language and in historical understanding; we have yet to deal explicitly with art as a mode or experience of truth.

In some ways the exposition of *Truth and Method* could have started with a discussion of art and 'aesthetic consciousness' because the first of the three main sections of this work starts with precisely this question: the problematical question of truth in relation to art. Gadamer's strategy in discussing art is not specifically to outline the nature of the beautiful or establish the philosophical basis for the different concepts of art; he wants to demonstrate quite simply that art is a form of truth about the world and not a heightened state of individual feeling. Art is not an innocent diversion and amusement but a crucial point of access to fundamental truths about the world and what it is to be human. Art uncovers truths about ourselves that no amount of scientific endeavour can reveal. Here Gadamer draws upon the rich romantic tradition in literature.

This position is highly controversial as there is a counter-tendency in the history of philosophy putting art and truth at opposing ends of a spectrum. Art here is often downgraded to the status of ornamentation and amusement, enriching life as a form of entertainment but in no way contributing to a profound understanding of the world.

On this view of art as amusement, it panders to emotions and feelings and can never rise to the dizzy heights of philosophical insight and scientific truth. A central figure in the history of philosophy responsible for a rather more sophisticated version of this attitude is Plato. More contentiously, the German philosopher and aesthetician Immanuel Kant has been placed by some in the same camp. Despite Kant's assertion that art and beauty give access to otherwise hidden truths about the way we are, Gadamer questions the truth status of art as it develops out of the Kantian tradition of aesthetics.

Plato's *Republic* is clearly the historical starting point for the view that all art is untruth. Plato puts into the mouth of Socrates the view that art deceitfully sells itself as truth but is in fact dangerously distorting, depending upon *mimesis* ('imitation') or rather misrepresentation when compared to the incorruptible knowledge of the philosophers. For Plato, philosophical wisdom is the only highway to truth; philosophers, by virtue of their direct and undistorted knowledge through apprehension of the Forms, have an unmediated grasp of the varying degrees of reality. The artists, on the other hand, the poets, dramatists and painters, deal not in truth but illusion. Theirs is a distorted and refracted world of subjective feeling and distortion since there is no recourse to the guiding hand of reason. They depend upon the tricks of perspective, in the case of the visual artists, and cheap manipulation of emotions, in the case of the dramatists.

The view of the artist advanced in the *Republic* is that there existed a rivalry between artists and philosophers, both setting themselves up as purveyors of truth and wisdom. Whether Plato, the supreme artist, whose philosophy is always couched in terms of parables and metaphors, is being ironic or playful when debunking art, is a much-disputed point; nevertheless, he inaugurates a tradition of philosophical suspicion of all forms of artistry, especially when it parades as access to the realm of the real. From the time of Plato onwards philosophy displayed a certain self-confidence that the antagonism with art had resulted in victory and the battle for truth had been settled once and for all. However, it is in more recent times that discussion of the truth status of art is, after Heidegger's notorious intervention, once more on the philosophical agenda but for Gadamer art once again is not given its full due.

In the modern period, the status of art as a form of truth is under attack from a new direction. Paradoxically, with the development of the newly created discipline called aesthetics[1] in the eighteenth century, Gadamer sees an implicit attack upon the idea of art as truth once again. Kant's Third Critique (*The Critique of Aesthetic Judgement*), an extremely influential contribution to debates about the nature of art, works on the assumption that art is fundamentally concerned with feeling.[2] For Gadamer, this constitutes an essential 'subjectivization' of art, for art is reduced to some variety of personal[3] experience and thus fails to rise above the level of feeling. In order to associate art with the more ennobled truth, Gadamer needs to be able to show that art is capable of something of greater significance than the power to engender delight or terror. Ultimately, in claiming truth for art, Gadamer wants to change the emphasis away from the aesthetic consumer to the nature of the artistic product itself, and what that artefact is able to disclose or open up. To make that kind of a move, Gadamer turns to his mentor Heidegger, specifically Heidegger's famous lectures on the nature of art, for it is here that a radical turn in philosophical writing about art takes place. These lectures of Heidegger given in Frankfurt in 1936 were attended by Gadamer and were later published as *The Origin of the Work of Art.*[4] This radical approach to art's origins and meaning had a profound effect upon Gadamer and the central ideas formed the basis for his subsequent work on artistic production; it was also to influence the future course of his philosophical hermeneutics, which depends so heavily upon the Heideggerian idea of art as a primordial engagement with truth. Against the view that art gives access to a range of uniquely 'aesthetic' feelings (what Gadamer terms 'aesthetic consciousness'), Heidegger spoke of the being of art in an utterly novel and new way.

For Heidegger, art is disclosive, and in this sense is truthful. Truth needs to be understood in its Heideggerian sense before we can connect it to art. The mainstream philosophical tradition tends to speak of truth as a kind of correctness whereby the mind corresponds rationally or empirically to the nature of the world. Correspondence or correctness is just one way, for Heidegger, of appropriating the Greek term for truth, *aletheia*; another sense of the word has more to do with bringing out of unconcealment or disclosure. In other words, art for Heidegger, like truth itself, is an opening up on to the world. Art discloses.

In the *Origin* essays Heidegger goes on to illustrate different forms of disclosure with reference to three examples: a painting, 'Shoes of the Peasant', from Van Gogh; a Greek temple; and lyric verse. The authentic interpretation of the peasant shoes, for Heidegger, has more to do with the nature (the being) and positioning of the shoes, setting up a form of play between Earth (nature) and World (human culture), than anything one may say about the feelings of pathos or nostalgia the picture may evoke in the gallery-viewer. The shoes, the focal point of the picture, more than anything else, Heidegger suggests, takes the viewer right into the world of the peasant.[5] Here is part of Heidegger's description, evoking the reality of the shoes and their place in the peasant world:

> From the dark opening of the worn insides of the shoes the toilsome tread of the worker stares forth. In the stiffly rugged heaviness of the shoes there is the accumulated tenacity of her slow trudge through the far-spreading and ever-uniform furrows of the field swept by a raw wind. On the leather lie the dampness and richness of the soil. Under the soles stretches the loneliness of the field-path as evening falls. In the shoes vibrates the silent call of the earth, its quiet gift of the ripening grain and its unexplained self-refusal in the fallow desolation of the wintry field.[6]

This is what he means by disclosure; the painting of the peasant shoes reveals a fundamental truth or truths about the life and world of the peasant. Consistent with Heidegger's general account of truth disclosure often works with its privation or opposite, concealment; as light is cast on one particular aspect of being, another immediately withdraws from view. Art, like other forms of truth, has the capacity to both reveal and conceal.

ART AS PLAY

Play, as an essential aspect of art, is of great significance for Gadamer. This idea, although important in the tradition of German aesthetic theory, notably in Schiller and Kant and after, does not come directly from these sources, for Gadamer. He looks to the anthropological work of the Dutch cultural historian Huizinga.[7] Although Huizinga charts the historical importance of play in all aspects of cultural life, Gadamer transforms play into a central feature of art.[8]

What does he mean by play? As well as obvious instances of play in organized sports, Gadamer has in mind the actual phenomenon of play in its endless variety, including metaphorical senses: 'the play of light, the play of the waves, the play of gears or parts of machinery, the interplay of limbs, the play of forces, the play of gnats, even a play on words' (*TM*, p. 103). Despite their differences, what these aspects of play all share in common is a 'to-and-fro movement that is not tied to any goal that would bring it to an end' (*TM*, p. 103). Play is an activity that is not random and yet has no obvious goal or teleological endpoint; purposeful and yet without some grand overarching purpose. And a to-and-fro movement is evident in all ball games where the ball is constantly in motion, providing the character of the play itself. No one knows how the game will end: it is given to sudden reversals of fortune, to the element of surprise as it shocks and unsettles expectations. Play is not necessarily light-hearted, as it clearly is in the operation of pastimes; in fact play can often start as a simple diversion and suddenly become deadly serious when winning or losing becomes a 'matter of life and death', as we say, albeit metaphorically, but with serious intent. Play is a constant to-and-fro movement and Gadamer focuses on this incessant back and forth motion because it reveals something about the nature of art as being essentially incomplete and incompletable. The meaning of art works is what is revealed and opened up in the constant oscillation between art work and interpreter. The meaning of the art work is never final, just as a game never reaches true finality; the game can always be played again and again and players will always be drawn into its horizon.

What Gadamer also wants to emphasize with the notion of play is how art is more than the heightened state of feeling or 'aesthetic consciousness' emphasized by much post-Kantian aesthetics. We need to take account of two relationships at work in the operation of play. On the one hand, there is the dynamic between the players and the game, while on the other there is the relationship between the players and the spectators, what Gadamer terms a 'playing along with'.[9] Concerning the players and the game, the game always takes precedence over the individual players. Sure enough teams will always have their star players and key individuals who gain glory for personal achievements, but the team, and more importantly the game itself, wherein the play is enacted, will always be more extensive than the actions of the players. This is a direct comment on the limitations of subjectivity.

Gadamer draws an analogy between forms of understanding and the individual. In subsuming the individual players to the greater structure of the team or the game itself, Gadamer echoes the earlier attack on subjectivity where individual reflection is a fragment of larger hermeneutical structures ('the closed circuits of historical life'), those of language and tradition.

All art and artistry in some way draws upon play. Mention has already been made of the obvious play of a team game. In a drama presentation, that is, a 'play', the audience is essential to the performance in the same way as spectators make a necessary contribution to a football match; for example, the spectators contribute something to the character of the game. Gadamer also refers to dancing, pointing out that the German word for play, *Spiel*, originally meant 'dance' (*TM*, p. 103). Dancing seems to be a clear illustration of the to-and-fro play already mentioned; a patterned activity, which yet remains unpredictable as to development and eventual outcome. Music is also a form of play, the most obvious sense of which is captured in the everyday expression 'to *play* a musical instrument'. The playfulness of the visual arts is perhaps less obvious and rather more difficult to grasp in the first instance, but on reflection a plausible explanation is something along these lines.

A painting draws the viewer into the world of the picture and the interaction with the viewer is playful in the sense that there is a to-and-fro dynamic between art work and viewer. We have already spoken of the way the work of art offers the viewer a world, a horizon of meaning; this we saw in relation to Heidegger. The painting invites and draws the viewer into its own world and the viewer is engaged in a constant activity of interrogating that world. The meaning of the painting is never fully disclosed as it is always the world of the painting as it engages in dialogue with the world of the viewer. As we can see, the art work operates in Gadamer as just another partner in a hermeneutical dialogue. Just as truth is essentially dialogue so too is art and its truth.

ART AS SYMBOL AND FESTIVAL

Two other aspects of art, symbol and festival, supplement play in Gadamer's aesthetics after *Truth and Method*, and these are outlined in the essay 'The relevance of the beautiful'.[10] Symbol is understood initially in its Greek original. In the ancient world a symbol was one piece of a broken object given to a guest. The other matching piece was kept by the provider of hospitality in the hope that if the two met in future 'the two pieces could be fitted together again to form a whole in an act of recognition'; consequently, 'the symbol represented something like a sort of pass used in the ancient world: something in and through which we recognize something already known to us'.[11] In some rather obscure way the relationship between the possessors of the broken object is replicated in the connection between the art work and the perceiver. Another example Gadamer gives from the classical world comes from Plato's *Symposium* where Aristophanes, the playwright, tells us that

> [O]riginally all human beings were spherical creatures. But later on, on account of their misbehaviour, the gods cut them in two. Thereafter, each of the halves, which originally belonged to one complete living being, seeks to be made whole once again. Thus every individual is a fragment or a *symbolon tou anthropou*.[12]

Gadamer is rather elusive on the full applicability of these analogies to his sense of 'symbol' but his meaning seems to be something along these lines. The meaning of the art work is not conditioned by or reducible to a story about its historical placing or its positioning within a specific artistic genre. The meaning of the art work is inscrutable and not immediately apparent; nevertheless, we turn to the work of art, in our search for the significance of our own lives, as if the work of art is going to complete the puzzle of existence in the way that the matching objects link together in an act of recognition as in the first illustration. What Gadamer seems to be getting at is that the art work, although symbolic, does not represent something else, or stand for a hidden meaning that needs to be cashed in or explained. The art work displays itself, but as symbol is a vehicle for attempted acts of self-recognition. We seek to understand ourselves in the art work; this is why art captivates and intrigues, drawing us into its world, however seemingly remote and distant that world at first appears. Gadamer warns against using the art work as symbolic in the sense of having a hidden code that we must crack in order to make sense of the work's hidden 'message'. On the contrary, what you see is what you get, the art work says what it says through what it discloses, but this is always something more than the perceiver can take account of and acknowledge. The meaning of the art work is never complete as we will always be able to recognize new things within it. The art work reveals aspects of a human world and its limitations just as much as we reveal aspects of the world of the art work (and its imitations) in an uneasy – because constantly changing – totality. The true *being* of the work of art will never be fully grasped; there will always be an aura of uniqueness and irreplaceability surrounding works of art.[13]

Gadamer also speaks of the art work as festive in the sense of being bound up with the celebration and remembering of festivals. If the notion of 'symbol' points to the being of the work of art, the notion of festival is more obviously aimed at revealing its temporality, its relationship to the time of its reception and the notion of time the celebration demonstrates. In the essay 'The festive character of theatre', Gadamer asks about the meaning of festivals and gives the following response:

> Festivals are to be celebrated. But what is the festive character of a festival? Naturally, this quality need not always be associated with joy or happiness, since in mourning we also share this festive character together. But a festive occasion is always something uplifting which raises the participants out of their everyday existence and elevates them into a kind of universal communion.[14]

The raising up and out of everyday existence is obviously something the participants experience and it is made possible through the festival's appropriation of its own temporality; it has the effect of suspending the everyday experience of time and this has the effect of injecting a note of mystery to the event. Gadamer illustrates his point by referring to the festival of Christmas. Here is a festival that celebrates an event that happened more than two thousand years ago and yet it happens every year and even so every Christmas celebration is different.

The festival creates its own time, which bursts through the mundane clock time of the diurnal and the everyday. Art is festive in the sense that it too disrupts and dislocates our everyday experience of time; it lifts us out of our daily routines and offers the opportunity to imagine ourselves and our engagements with the world differently.

> It is of the nature of the festival that it should proffer time, arresting it and allowing it to tarry. That is what festive celebration means. The calculating way in which we normally manage and dispose of time is, as it were, brought to a standstill.[15]

The Heideggerian idea of 'tarrying' is important here for Gadamer. Art, like the festival, offers the opportunity to take stock of one's life, to reflectively and deliberatively think one's lifetime differently.

As the example of mourning above testifies, the festival is also an act of sharing. The festival binds and brings together the community in more intimate and important ways than other experiences of solidarity and togetherness. And the community need not be localized and parochial; Gadamer gives the example of witnessing Greek antiquities in the National Museum of Athens. He speaks of being 'overcome by an all-embracing festive quiet' and notes that one 'senses how everyone is gathered together for something'.[16] In marvelling at ancient Greek artefacts, one is experiencing the sense in which all participants are part of a common historical and cultural heritage. The notion of tradition is important again here. Gadamer suggests that great art binds in so far as we experience ourselves as a larger whole, a part of Western culture and a part of a common humanity.

Art is truthful because it, like other forms of dialogue, 'says something to someone'.[17] But because the experience of art is the experience of meaning it demonstrates that art is ultimately subordinate to, because part of, hermeneutics. As Gadamer says, 'Aesthetics must be swallowed up in hermeneutics.'[18]

GADAMER'S POETIC TURN[19]

Gadamer's writings after *Truth and Method* elaborate upon and extend the diverse claims of philosophical hermeneutics. In some of these later essays and lectures, emphasis is laid upon the practical application of basic hermeneutical insights to areas as diverse as education[20] and modern medical practice.[21] But another important preoccupation after *Truth and Method* is a sustained focus upon the aesthetics, and aesthetic uses, of language, more specifically upon the poetic. Linguisticality, as a prominent feature of our relationship to the world, was worked out in detail in *Truth and Method*, and Part Three, 'The ontological shift of hermeneutics guided by language', culminates in a final declaration, which in some ways the whole work leads up to, that 'Being that can be understood is language' (*TM*, p. 474). Although hints are evident in the final pages of *Truth and Method*, Gadamer finds the most undistorted affirmations of being in poetry, particularly in the modern lyric. Writings on the general nature of poetic language and its connections to ordinary, religious and philosophical language are collected in the volume *The Relevance of the Beautiful* (Gadamer, 1986b). Gadamer also produced a number of interpretive essays on the poetry and poetics of Rilke, George and Celan, many of which are now translated.[22] What distinguishes everyday discourse from poetry? A good deal turns on the distinction between 'everyday' or 'ordinary' and 'poetic' language. Gadamer's increasing appreciation of the poetic leads him into interpretations of contemporary poetry, notably the hermetic lyric. 'Play' and 'play-fulness', discussed in the First Part of *Truth and Method* as hidden or repressed aspects of the truth of the work of art, work most emphat-ically in the realm of the poetic. When hermeneutically reclaimed, poetic play works against subjectivist, modernist, versions of the aesthetic of feeling, already discussed in the section 'Art as play'. Gadamer, on his own admission, fails, in *Truth and Method*, to fully thematize poetic play as it warrants no more than a few passing men-tions in Parts Two and Three of *Truth and Method*, losing itself in the interpretive turn towards those other facets of hermeneutic truthful-ness, historicality and language itself. In the later essays, specifically those reflecting upon the poetic and the aesthetic, 'play' becomes wider and assumes a much greater significance. Play, and this is most evident in the language of poetry, becomes a fundamental character-istic of language itself.

Notions of 'play' and 'language-games' are more obviously associated, in the analytical tradition, with the later work of Wittgenstein, as noticed in earlier chapters. For all his appreciation of language's specificity, Wittgenstein seldom thematizes poetic lan-guage. There is little explicit rumination on the poetic uses of lan-guage in Wittgenstein's later work other than occasional gnomic asides in the *Investigations* and elsewhere.

The Wittgensteinian silence about the poetic is significant. The attempt to move away from a logic-driven picture theory of meaning in the *Tractatus* to the more informal, loosely textured, pragmatics of language in the *Investigations* represents a return to 'Wittgenstein's rough ground' of ordinary language. But the picture of a full living language is still incomplete without the rhetorical and metaphorical voices. More than embellishments, they are the lifeblood of everyday speech and writing as the search for ever-new meanings emerge from the tradition. Nowhere is this more evident than in the quest for per-sonal meanings in the poetic, where ordinary language is unhinged from its everyday patterns and finds ever-new modes of expression. The inner flexibility of language-games, their capacity to transform and extend themselves, to work in new uncharted regions, is an aspect of the poetic largely unheeded by Wittgenstein.

Despite the poverty of explicit reference to the poetic, the thought occurs that Wittgenstein is not totally unaware of the poetic dimension. The move to an increasingly compressed and aphoristic style, the whole thrust of the later work as an exercise in freeing up language, may be a point of entry for considering an indirect engagement with the poetic. Wittgenstein's complex relationship to the figurative will be re-visited in the light of Gadamer's treatment of everyday and poetic language.

GADAMER ON ORDINARY, EVERYDAY LANGUAGE

In the essay 'Philosophy and Poetry'[23] Gadamer draws a striking analogy between words and money:

> [Valéry] contrasted the *poetic* word with the *everyday* use of language in a striking comparison that alludes to . . . the gold standard: *everyday language* resembles small change which, like our own paper money, does not actually possess the value that it symbolizes. The gold coins . . . on the other hand, actually possessed as metal the value that was imprinted upon them. In a similar way, the language of poetry is not a mere pointer that refers to something else, but like the gold coin, is what it represents.[24]

In another reference to the same Valéry conceit, in 'Composition and Interpretation'[25] Gadamer claims that 'ordinary language resembles a coin that we pass round among ourselves in place of something else' and, 'everyday language . . . *points to something beyond* itself and *disappears* behind it' (Gadamer, 1986).[26] Returning to the gold analogy in later life Gadamer says in the 'Reflections' essay, 'language emerges in its full autonomy . . . language just stands for itself: it brings itself to stand before us.' Whereas, 'Ordinary language resembles a coin that we pass round among ourselves in place of something else', he claims, 'poetic language is like gold itself' (Hahn, 1997, p. 39).

Just as paper money is only valuable to the extent that it is underwritten by something of intrinsic worth, gold,[27] so the ordinary word 'does not actually possess the value that it symbolizes'. There are possible ambiguities lurking here. Does the analogy suggest that ordinary words have no value without poetic words (and the meanings of ordinary words change as poetic words change)? Or is the assumption that ordinary words are of inferior value because they are no more than tokens, whereas poetic language is what it is? Ambiguity aside, the purpose of the analogy is to suggest that in the everyday uses of language the words themselves (as sounds and structured patterns of meaning) are a medium, through which pass the matters at issue, the subject matter of the exchange. On the other hand, the poetic word does not disappear behind the matter at issue but is manifest as the matter at issue itself.

What can we say of the *disappearance* of language? In rejecting an account of meaning based upon the truth-functionality of propositions, Gadamer looks to the mutuality of understanding, to the 'fusion of the horizons', as he termed it in *Truth and Method* (pp. 306–7 and 374–5). Meaning is not something self-sufficient or standing over and above words. Participation in the creation of meaning accompanies the very act of speaking. Because ultimately every assertion is an answer to an implied or actual question, meaning conforms not to the logic of the proposition but to the 'logic of question and answer'(*TM*, pp. 369–79). Although language is regulated by sometimes strict, sometimes loose, semantic rules, it is flexible enough in its application to generate possibilities overreaching and extending the original rules. In ordinary language this self-transformation is minimal and unnoticed. Language is at its most transparent when the logic of question and answer is at its least searching and understanding at its least problematical, in the routine exchanges of everyday conversation, for example. The situation dramatically changes when the opaque self-presentation of poetic language disrupts and complicates the normally smooth flow of understanding.

Living language requires more than conformity to semantic rules, as Chapter 5 established. To understand and make ourselves understood is also an ethical matter. 'Good will' even comes into play;[28] echoing Donald Davidson's principle of charity,[29] Gadamer assumes a hermeneutics of trust (against the 'hermeneutics of suspicion') and a willingness to accommodate the voice of the other: 'Social life depends upon our acceptance of everyday speech as trustworthy; we cannot order a taxi without this trust. Thus understanding is the average case not misunderstanding', he says in an interview entitled 'Writing and the Living Voice' (Gadamer, 1992, pp. 63–71). As an explicit riposte to deconstruction he continues, 'And Derrida, for example, when he takes a different view (presumably that *mis-understanding* rather than understanding is the average case) is speaking about literature. In literature there is a struggle to bring something into expression beyond what is accepted' (ibid., p. 71). 'The struggle . . . beyond what is accepted' is what literature in general and poetry in particular engages in as an expansion of the meanings of the everyday.

Evidently poetic language is not limited to the language of poetry, although poetry – especially modern, hermetic, lyric poetry – is language at its most poetic.

Gadamer constructs a kind of literary hierarchy 'ascending from lyric poetry through epic and tragedy . . . leading to the novel and any demanding prose' (Gadamer, 1986b, p. 136). Attention is drawn, not simply to a literary taxonomy, but to degrees of interpretation and translatability. The language of the novel, being close to the structures of everyday speech, is the least problematic, as it minimally draws upon interpretive resources and depends on the kind of trust underpinning everyday transactions (like hailing a taxi). At the other extreme, the lyric poem flatly resists easy transliteration. 'No translation of a lyric poem ever conveys the original work', he observes in the essay 'On the contribution of poetry to the search for truth'.[30] 'The best we can hope for is that one poet should come across another and put a new poetic work, as it were, in place of the original by creating an equivalent with the materials of a different language' (Gadamer, 1986b, p. 111).

THE POEM AS 'EMINENT TEXT'

Frequently Gadamer speaks of 'eminence' as a quality of poetic works. Here, 'poetic compositions are text in a new kind of sense: they are text in an *eminent* sense of the word . . . In this kind of text language emerges in its full autonomy. Here language just stands for itself: it brings itself to stand before us'.[31] The poetic word is eminent. It literally sticks out, protrudes in the literal sense (e-minent).

In ordinary language, words disappear into their functionality, vanishing in the face of the matters at issue. In poetic language, words take on a life of their own, in this sense. In ordinary language, the language of 'the homeland' referred to by Gadamer,[32] we are more attentive to the 'message' than the 'medium'. But with the poetic, the word's 'corporeality', as Gerald Bruns terms it,[33] shines forth. The physicality of words, through their sounds, modulation, tonality, tempo, dynamics, superfluous factors in the exchange of information of everyday speech, come to the fore in the poetic utterance. The poetic word, in transcending mere information, disrupts the everyday (and our situatedness within it). In *Truth and Method* Gadamer points to a hermeneutical experience of 'being pulled up short' (*TM*, p. 268) in an encounter with a text. We are suddenly alienated from the text's meaning as it thwarts our expectations. The experience of novelty with a text is dramatically heightened in the lyric poem.

In ordinary language there is invariably an element of inventiveness present. All interpretation is production of meaning rather than straightforward reproduction (or, as I spoke of earlier with respect to rules, re-enactment). The constant turning of the 'hermeneutic circle' destabilizes meaning and shows it to be in motion, never unitary or foreclosed. This inventive, self-transformative quality is heightened and intensified in the poetic utterance and links in to the 'speculative' dimension of language. In lyric poetry particularly, Gadamer claims, 'the poet releases the multidimensionality of the associations of meaning which is suppressed by practical unity of intention in logically controlled, one-dimensional everyday speech'.[34] As if to demonstrate the truth of his claim, Gadamer, in his essay 'Who am I and who are you?', a reading of Paul Celan's poetic cycle 'Breath turn' or 'Breathcrystal' (*Atemkristall*), analyses the ways in which the reader's sense of individuation and personal identity is disoriented and unsettled in the engagement with these verses. He says, 'We do not know at the outset, on the basis of any distanced overview or preview, what *I* or *You* means here (in Celan's poems) or whether I is the I of the poet referring to himself, or the I that is each of us, this is what we must learn'.[35] The whole question of who is addressing whom in the decontextualized zone of the poetic, where language is effectively unhinged from its customary sites, raises important questions for philosophical hermeneutics. With the usual semantic reference points distorted and dislocated in the poem the hermeneutical task is more demanding, as Gadamer admits. Words extend themselves, moving into new and hitherto unknown spaces in the tradition.

Meaning is ultimately a dialogue, a negotiation between poem and reader. 'In a poem', Gadamer says in the 'Reflections' essay, 'with *whom* does . . . communication take place? Is it with the reader? With which *reader*? Here the dialectic of question and answer which is always the basis of the hermeneutic and which corresponds to the basic structure of the dialogue undergoes a special modification' (Hahn, 1997, pp. 39–40). Quite what this special modification is he does not make explicit but he says, a little later in this essay, something worthy of note:

> As I look back today I see one point in particular where I did not achieve the theoretical consistency I strove for in *Truth and Method*. I did not make it clear enough how the . . . basic projects that were brought together in the concept of play harmonized. . . . On the one hand there is the orientation to the game we play with art and on the other the grounding of language in conversation, the game of language . . . I needed to unite the game of language more closely with the game art plays. (Hahn, 1997, pp. 41–2)

Poetic language is not the only instance of language at play for the playful element is never far away even in the routine enactments of daily conversation: yet it stands for language at its most playful. Gadamer succeeded in suggesting this in his historical survey of the origins and development of modern aesthetics, in Part One of *Truth and Method* (see particularly *TM*, pp. 101–11). Only in the later work, as he recently confessed, did he see how this 'playfulness' is a description of all linguistic activity, with language at its most ludic in the poetic. It is worth noting, especially when comparing Gadamer to Wittgenstein, that 'play' and 'playfulness' are not the same. Play could be taken as no more than regulated activity. On the other hand, playfulness resists codification; we might even say it is playful by virtue of the resistance to regulation. But play and playfulness are not just dimensions of life and language; they achieve a special status in art. All art, and here we include the poetic, is play, but here especially the activity of play always becomes more than itself in what Gadamer terms 'transformation into structure' (*TM*, p. 110). Play transforms the players and itself as it discloses some structural dimension of reality for 'the transformation is a transformation into the true' (*TM*, p. 112). Once again the idea of poetic play as disclosure, an opening up of the real, is emphasized.

This enriched notion of play puts Gadamer's account of language in a new light. Those who see in his work little more than a seamless monological and self-affirming (Hegelian) tradition, blind to difference and alterity, ignore his attempt to re-align the poetic in his hermeneutics. The playfulness of the hermeneutical dialogue, the fact that it can never make implicit meanings completely explicit, the fact that the unsaid is always more extensive than the said, indicate a constant measure of difference. The element of play in dialogue, eliminating the possibility of closure and identity, is strong evidence that alterity and difference outflanks identity of meaning in Gadamer. If this is the case, the reduction of Gadamer's hermeneutics to just another version of Hegelianism (in a more modern idiom) is questionable.

NOTES

1 Alexander Gottlieb Baumgarten (1714–62), German philosopher, invented the term *aesthetics* (from the Greek for 'perception by means of the senses') to describe the effects of art.
2 Albeit feeling with a rational basis.
3 The term 'intersubjective' might occur to some as a possible substitute for personal here. But does the idea of the intersubjective get beyond the subjective? Not so for Gadamer. In an interview with Carsten Dutt, Gadamer is asked, 'Wouldn't you say that hermeneutical philosophy thematises converzation as our capacity for rational intersubjectivity?' Gadamer responds, 'Oh, please spare me that completely misleading concept of intersubjectivity, of a subjectivism doubled!' (Gadamer, 2001, p. 59). Evoking *Homo* intersubjectivity never really overcomes the problem of the subjective. The move to solidarity in the later work is more obviously hermeneutical.
4 First published in 1950. For an abridged version of these lectures see 'The Origin of the Work of Art' in Krell (1978), pp. 144–87.
5 The idea of 'world' here is reminiscent of the notion of world (as opposed to 'environment') encountered in *Truth and Method*. In fact Gadamer's world and environment correspond very closely to Heidegger's World and Earth.
6 Krell (1978), p. 163.
7 In *Truth and Method* Gadamer acknowledges Johann Huizinga's *Homo Ludens* as the principal source for his account of 'play'. See *TM*, p. 104. Not withstanding the acknowledged debt to Huizinga, Gadamer's notion of play is in fact remarkably Kantian. For all the criticisms of the legacy of Kant's aesthetics, Gadamer conveniently forgets the description of play in the Third Critique, which is, in fact, very close to his own conception.
8 In Gadamer's writings after *Truth and Method*, the concept of play takes on greater significance; it best describes the nature of the relationship between language and language-users. The playful dimension to language is discussed in relation to Wittgenstein in Chapter 8.

9 Discussed in Gadamer (1986b), pp. 23–4.
10 Gadamer (1986b), pp. 3–53. This is also the title of the collection of essays on art and poetry and aesthetics generally.
11 Gadamer (1986b), p. 31.
12 Gadamer (1986b), pp. 31–2.
13 The notion of the aura Gadamer takes from Walter Benjamin's celebrated essay 'The work of art in the age of mechanical reproduction'.
14 Gadamer (1986b), p. 58.
15 Gadamer (1986b), p. 42.
16 Gadamer (1986b), p. 40.
17 Gadamer (2001), p. 70.
18 Gadamer (2001), p. 69.
19 A slightly different version of this and the next section are to be found in Lawn (2004), Chapter 7, 'Ordinary and extraordinary language: The hermeneutics of the poetic word'.
20 A selection of Gadamer's writings on education, specifically his work on the role of the university in modern life, is collected in Misgeld and Nicholson (1992).
21 The collection of essays *The Enigma of Health* adopts a critical attitude to modern medical practice. Gadamer traces modernity's increasing dependence upon technology and technological thinking to emphasize the eclipsing of the traditional (hermeneutical) idea of medicine as a healing *art*.
22 For a collection of essays on Gadamer's interpretations of the poetry of Paul Celan see Gadamer (1997). The introductory essay in this volume, 'The remembrance of language: An introduction to Gadamer's poetics', by G. L. Bruns, is a useful overview of Gadamer's turn to poetry and introduction to his readings of Celan's difficult verse. For an essay on Rilke see Gadamer's 'Mytho-poetic inversion in Rilke's *Duino Elegies*' in Gadamer (1994). Other essays on poetry are to be found in Misgeld and Nicholson (1992), 'Hermeneutics, poetry, and modern culture', pp. 63–131.
23 Gadamer (1986b), pp. 131–9.
24 Gadamer (1986b), p. 132; my emphasis.
25 Gadamer (1986b), pp. 66–73.
26 Heidegger uses a similar analogy in the essay 'On the Essence of Truth' (Krell, 1978, pp. 117–41).
27 The gold standard no longer exists but the analogy still stands. Marxist economists would take issue with the idea of gold having an intrinsic value. The high value of gold is largely determined by the immense amount of congealed labour within it.
28 Derrida's third of his 'Three Questions to Gadamer' in the 1981 Paris 'encounter' concerns 'the underlying structure of good will'. See Michelfelder and Palmer (1989).
29 'Charity in interpreting the words . . . of others is unavoidable . . . just as we must maximize the sense of what the alien is talking about, so we must maximize the self-consistency we attribute to him, on pain of not understanding *him*' (from 'Truth and Meaning', p. 27, in Davidson, 1984).

30 Gadamer (1986b), pp. 105–15.
31 Hahn (1997), p. 39. Also see the essay, 'The eminent text and its truth', Gadamer (1980b), pp. 3–23.
32 In the essay 'The language of metaphysics' Gadamer asks, 'Is not language always the language of the homeland and the process of becoming-at-home in the world?' (Gadamer, 1994, p. 78).
33 Gadamer (1997), pp. 2–11.
34 'Meaning and the Concealment of Meaning', in Gadamer (1997), p. 167.
35 Gadamer (1997), p. 70.

CHAPTER 7

THE LATER GADAMER

AFTER *TRUTH AND METHOD*

This chapter traces some of the developments and refinements in Gadamer's thought after *Truth and Method*. The basic insights of this central Gadamerian text endure throughout his later work but there are distinct changes in emphasis. One modification is an almost imperceptible slip from talk of tradition to that of solidarity. This chapter examines Gadamer's understanding of the term solidarity and the consequences for hermeneutics, by way of a comparison with the concept as it is used in Richard Rorty's essay of the same name.[1]

In tandem with these changes, an increasingly dominant motif throughout the later period (after 1960) is an emphasis upon the hermeneutical dimension of the various forms of actual practice. Some critics have referred to this turn in Gadamer's work as a move to 'applied hermeneutics'. This chapter will discuss briefly the application of hermeneutics to three of the areas of practice identified in the later work, these being the role of the expert in modern society, the character of medical practice and the nature of the modern university. Not only does Gadamer succeed in highlighting the hermeneutical dimension to practice, he, contrary to the voices of his critics, is able to offer a powerful critique of existing practices. The canard that philosophical hermeneutics is an uncritical celebration of the *status quo* and, like Wittgenstein's view of philosophy, 'leaves the world as it is' is here laid to rest. This theme of the absence or presence to a critical edge to philosophical hermeneutics we will discuss in more detail in the final chapter.

GADAMER AND RORTY ON SOLIDARITY

There does not appear to be a single reference to the notion of solidarity in the whole of *Truth and Method*. Yet in the many subsequent essays and interviews the concept is given more and more attention.[2] In many of the desultory interviews with Gadamer on matters of politics, ethics and world affairs, it is frequently discussed. Significantly, during the period after 1960, the references to tradition, occupying such a central role in *Truth and Method*, seem to vanish from the lexicon. This gives rise to the suggestion that the idea of solidarity becomes either a replacement for the earlier 'tradition', or a way of amplifying and expanding upon it. In many ways the suggestion of a move from one to the other has a certain logical plausibility. Tradition, as already outlined, is the conduit through which flow the central elements of social life, connecting past to present and future. All interpretation takes place against the background of a constantly changing tradition and yet tradition itself is based upon deep-seated agreements, and it would be possible to equate that agreement with a form of solidarity.

The dictionary defines solidarity as a 'unity or agreement of feeling or action, especially among individuals with a common interest' (*Concise Oxford Dictionary*). This is consistent with an established view of tradition since for Gadamer one of tradition's principal features is a commonality and implicit structure of agreements, which provide the essential backdrop for understanding. Language and history are largely synonymous with tradition. In the same way, language and history presuppose forms of solidarity. But solidarity is not just a background agreement; it is often more, being part of an agenda of political and ethical aspirations for the future. Although tradition depends upon solidarity there is often the hope that solidarities can be extended and expanded. It is in this more utopian sense of hope that Gadamer's solidarity moves in the later work. In order to appreciate the way it operates in later Gadamer a comparison with the work of Richard Rorty seems appropriate. Rorty famously turns to solidarity, especially in the collection of essays *Contingency, Irony and Solidarity*.[3] I want to suggest that Gadamer's use of solidarity is actually much richer and more plausible than that given by Rorty. Not only this, but Gadamer's solidarity is an arguable basis for a programme of ethical and political values overcoming the evidently nihilistic Rortyan dependence upon pure contingency. This, of course, was the point of Rorty's turn to solidarity, to move to some sort of quasi-ethical site without resort to essentialist or transcendent claims.

In the essay 'Solidarity',[4] Rorty aims to establish a basis for ethical commitment whilst sticking doggedly to some version of contingency and avoidance of a story about the grounding of ethical principles in metaphysics or transcendence. Rorty's Wittgensteinian pragmatism, not unlike Gadamerian hermeneutics, rejects any form of non-contingent, non-historical, footing in human nature and prohibits any resort to abstract and non-specific talk of a common humanity or a human essence. Yet despite rejecting a non-historical grounding he sees in a commitment to solidarity ethical possibilities, including what he terms 'moral progress', an idea impossible to justify in terms of contingency alone.

The extent and degree of solidarity can be gauged empirically. Rorty gives the following controversial example:

> If you were a Jew in the period when the trains were running to Auschwitz, your chances of being hidden by your gentile neighbours were greater if you lived in Denmark or Italy than if you lived in Belgium . . . a way of describing this difference is by saying that many Danes and Italians showed a sense of human solidarity which many Belgians lacked.[5]

And:

> Consider . . . those Danes and those Italians. Did they say, about their Jewish neighbours that they deserved to be saved because they were human beings? Perhaps sometimes they did, but surely they would usually, if queried, have used more parochial terms to explain why they were taking risks to protect a given Jew – e.g., that this particular Jew was a fellow Milanese, or a fellow Jutlander, or a fellow member of the same union or profession.[6]

What the Danes and Italians did, and the Belgians apparently did not, is actively expand and advance their ideas of solidarity. Moral progress is described in this way as a willingness to extend inclusiveness, 'in the direction of greater human solidarity . . . the ability to see more and more traditional differences (of tribe, religion, race, customs and the like) as unimportant when compared with similarities with respect to pain and humiliation – the ability to think of people wildly different from ourselves as included in the range of "us" '.[7]

Here an appreciation of the contingency of things excludes the possibility of appealing to a common humanity or the human essence: moral progress is piecemeal and incremental and made possible by building upon existing solidarities and imagining greater ones. Solidarity with urban blacks in the US, for Rorty, starts from an appreciation that they are first and foremost 'fellow Americans'[8] rather than more abstract 'human beings' or parts of a 'common humanity'. Moral advance is made not by virtue of an appeal to an abstract universal law or essentialist humanity but to imagining the possibility of an ever-widening circle of solidarities.

What authorizes solidarities if appeals to factors beyond the limitations of contingent linguistic communities are ruled out? Rorty cites abhorrence of cruelty and humiliation ('the worst things we do') as the bottom line. And what provides the motivation for increased solidarity? He looks to literary imagination – as expressed in the novels of Vladimir Nabokov and George Orwell, for example – to inspire hope, self-creation and new and expanded forms of consensus and agreement. To advance and strengthen solidarities we need to create new narratives and pictures of our own possibilities.

There is a problem here. When Rorty speaks of an abhorrence of cruelty and humiliation he is moving perilously close to affirming the very position he is trying to avoid. The rejection of cruelty, if it is to have any force, needs to be a universal trait and this militates against the kind of contingency upon which social life is built. Yet there is something entirely plausible and admirable about Rorty's desire to construct an ethics of solidarity from nothing more than the bare essentials, that is, the contingent agreements of human life. One cannot but secretly applaud his wish to do away with the smoke and mirrors of metaphysics and theology, on which appeals to enriched ethical life often depend.

Does Rorty's position make sense? Norman Geras in *Solidarity and the Conversation of Humankind: The Ungroundable Liberalism of Richard Rorty*[9] thinks not. He takes Rorty to task on empirical and theoretical grounds. Geras clings on to the idea of a universal human nature. As a committed Marxist it is to the Sixth Thesis on Feuerbach, proclaiming the human essence as 'the ensemble of social relations', he looks for an alternative. The empirical grounds Rorty refers to in his claim about the local and the parochial are contested. On the basis of intensive trawls through Holocaust literature and the testimonies of the 'Righteous among the nations', and the less exalted individuals responsible for saving Jewish lives, Geras tells a story at odds with the Rorty version. He claims that frequently the rescuers appealed to precisely the things Rorty plays down, that is, a common humanity and being human, as such.

Let us now contrast Rorty's version of solidarity to the one offered by Gadamer. For him, solidarities are revealed, reclaimed and uncovered within the fabric of language and tradition before they are created, imagined and invented. It is at this point that the two positions most evidently diverge. Whereas Rorty speaks of the solidarities in terms of 'creation' and 'invention', Gadamer looks to the need to mine existing resources, with the thought that they may be hermeneutically retrieved. In conversation with Karsten Dutt, Gadamer opposes 'invention' to 'awareness'. At one point we get the following claim: 'We do not need to invent . . . solidarities', he says, 'we merely have to make ourselves aware of them'.[10]

Rorty sets up a similar tension between 'creation' and 'recognition':

> The right way to construe the slogan ['We have obligations to human beings simply as such'] is as urging us to *create* a more expansive sense of solidarity than we presently have. The wrong way is to think of it as urging us to *recognize* such a solidarity, as something that exists antecedently to our recognition of it.[11]

It is the utopian vision of 'strong poets' and 'liberal ironists' with the foresight to envisage new final narratives of solidarity Rorty reveres. Moral horizons are expanded paradigmatically through the literary expression of hope and an increased abhorrence of cruelty and humiliation. But for all the rhetorical appeal of Rorty's position he depends upon the thinly textured voluntaristic acts of will of the 'strong textualists' and 'strong poets'. Both Gadamer and Rorty undercut the traditional groundings of ethics, making appeals to abstract universality redundant. In both cases their turn to solidarity is an attempt to rescue ethics from groundlessness and potential postmodern nihilism. Gadamer does not relapse into an affirmation of a common humanity but he is often adamant about the need to stress commonality rather than difference. He cedes the possibility that meanings are dispersed and deferred: 'Of course we encounter limits again and again: we speak past each other and are even at cross-purposes with ourselves.' However, the opacity and potential breakdown of meaning only occurs where some measure of agreement already exists. Failure to communicate would not be possible, Gadamer says, if 'we had not travelled a long way together . . . All human solidarity, all social stability, presupposes this'.[12] Such a comment would also apply to the hermeneutics of suspicion and the view that language inevitably falls victim to the hidden snares of ideology. Despite linguistic distortions through the intervening structures of power or class or gender or the vagaries of the unconscious, for the most part we need to accept that we have 'travelled a long way together' before we emphasize the degree to which we might travel apart.

Rorty's move from contingency to irony to solidarity is not fully convincing. The advantage of Gadamer's solidarities are that they are more solidly and deeply enmeshed within the (traditional) fabric of social life and offer a more realistic hope for expanding the forms of mutuality and commonality on which solidarity itself depends. Any resistance to what Charles Taylor calls the 'malaises' of modernity starts from an appreciation of Rorty's 'social hope' but needs something more: namely, the kind of ethical background I claim Gadamer provides in solidarity. The prospect of greater solidarity gives Gadamer's writings, in his final years, a degree of optimism. Apart from the apparent despair and incomprehension he evidently expressed regarding 9/11 – mentioned at the end of Chapter 1 – there is a constant theme of a secular hope for the future in Gadamer's later work,[13] strongly reminiscent of Ernst Bloch's *Principle of Hope*. 'One ought never to allow dogmatism to stifle utopian fantasy and readiness for reflection', says Gadamer,

> [E]ven when dogmatism gives itself the appearance of analytical sobriety. That is really very far from what I mean. What I also mean is that we can only protect and further develop solidarities on the broad basis of opinion culture that is not consciously steered by us – certainly not by the philosophers – but comes into existence by itself.[14]

Gadamer cites the protest movement against atomic power,[15] and the struggle to give legal protections to animals, nature and children,[16] as examples of genuine solidarities that give hope for the future.

APPLIED HERMENEUTICS

In the 'Foreword to the Second Edition' of *Truth and Method*[17] Gadamer answers the many critics who took issue with aspects of the original version of the work. Although the book was generally well received he felt the overall intent of the book had been misunderstood and that it was taken to be offering no more than a refinement of traditional hermeneutics. Concerning the purpose of the book, the following instructive comment is offered in the Foreword: 'My revival of the expression *hermeneutics*, with its long tradition, has apparently led to some misunderstanding.' He adds:

> I did not wish to elaborate a system of rules to describe, let alone, direct, the methodical procedure of the human sciences. Nor was it my aim to investigate the theoretical foundation of work in these fields in order to put my findings to practical ends.[18]

The impetus for the book was neither strictly practical nor theoretical, but philosophical: 'My real concern', he said, 'was and is philosophic: *not what we do or what we ought to do, but what happens to us over and above our wanting and doing.*'[19] The earlier biblical and legal hermeneutics gave normative guidance for the avoidance of incorrect interpretation. Gadamer's purpose is completely different. His work is philosophical in the phenomenological sense of accounting for what actually happens irrespective of 'our wanting and doing'; it is an enquiry into the nature of interpretation itself. He succeeds in establishing that all forms of understanding, in both practical life and with respect to the underpinnings of the human sciences, depend upon the hermeneutical movement already described in great detail in previous chapters. Although Gadamer's hermeneutics has no direct practical consequences, in the sense of offering guidance on the reading of specific texts, he establishes that the notion of application is at the heart of understanding itself, as the comment on what 'happens to us over and above our wanting and doing' emphasizes. Yet when seen from a hermeneutical perspective, many of our everyday practices take on a completely different aspect in this light. So in this way, philosophical hermeneutics does have practical dimensions since it can modify attitudes and practices and offers new perspectives on activities and practices hitherto unexamined and taken for granted.

This section focuses on 'applied hermeneutics'; a term used as the subtitle to a collection of essays on literary criticism, writings on the nature of the university, the future of Europe, the role of the expert in modern society, and much besides.[20] As the editors of this collection of essays say in their introduction, 'The essays . . . are not an application of hermeneutics that came after he wrote the theory down in *Truth and Method*.'[21] In other words, it would be completely misguided to take *Truth and Method* to be the grand theory and the later works to be its application to various regional areas of practice. Even in *Truth and Method* there is an acknowledgement that application is part of the whole process of hermeneutical understanding. This said, the later works of Gadamer are, more evidently than *Truth and Method*, engagements with practical activities in the life world, the actual world beyond the philosophy seminar room. This 'applied hermeneutics' covers such diverse areas of practice as education, literary criticism, psychoanalysis and medical practice. In the essay 'The limitations of the expert' Gadamer sees in modern cultural life an overemphasis upon the cult of specialization. In questioning the dependence in modern culture on the role of the expert, Gadamer is, once again, following Heidegger. Heidegger's rejection of science and modern technology is part of a much larger argument about the dominance of metaphysics. Effectively science and technology contribute to the tendency in modernity for the forgetting of the question of *being*.

Gadamer's preoccupation is not so much with being but the neglect of the power of tradition and solidarity in the modern age. Deference to the expert is only coherent when the commonalities outlined above are overridden. He says:

I am convinced that even in a highly bureaucratized, thoroughly organized and thoroughly specialized society, it is possible to strengthen existing solidarities. Our public life appears to me to be defective in so far as there is too much emphasis upon the different and disputed, upon that which is contested or in doubt. What we truly have in common and what unites us thus remains, so to speak, without a voice. Probably we are harvesting the fruits of a long training in the perception of differences and in the sensibility demanded by it. Our historical education aims in this direction, our political habits permit confrontations and the bellicose attitude to become commonplace. In my view we could only gain by contemplating the deep solidarities underlying all norms of human life.[22]

The suggestion here is that the differences in status, control and power in bureaucratized societies are made manifest through specialization. Specialization can be challenged in various ways. What is common for Gadamer is not a common humanity but the brute fact that specialist knowledge, the kind that inevitably gives rise to hierarchies and uneven social power, lacks authority, in the sense described in Chapter 2, where real authority springs from genuine knowledge. Concerning the dialogical nature of language and knowledge we need to remind ourselves that the kind of control of language and the world instrumental reason seeks is unrealizable. Gadamer's vision of language is one of a ceaseless conversation; an interminable dialogue that is under no individual or interest group's control. Dialogue as fallible and corrigible militates against this.

In keeping with the inheritance from German idealism, via Nietzsche and Heidegger, Gadamer rejects the scientific-technical world-view and reacts against the idea that scientific-technological specialism overshadows underlying solidarities. This theme is developed to great effect in the collection of essays on medical practice entitled *The Enigma of Health*.[23] He questions the idea of the medical practitioner as a specialist technologist of the body, preferring instead to retrieve the ancient sense of medicine as a hermeneutical art; that is, as a rather mysterious, interpretive, practice: after all, who really understands the body? The primordial sense of medical practice is not exemplified by the all-knowing doctor and the ignorant patient but through a more egalitarian solidarity – a hermeneutical relationship. When said and done the doctor does not control health but maintains a healing dialogue with the patient, leaving the rest to the 'open domain of nature'. In retrieving the vanishing sense of medical practice as a hermeneutical art, Gadamer offers a way of resisting the monolithic power of medical technology and the drug industry by questioning its monopoly on medical truth. In fact many alternative therapies have more in common with the authentic 'art of healing' being essentially interpretive, tentative and dialogical. The contemporary medical practitioner has access to the most sophisticated technology, whether it is life-support systems, the wherewithal for organ transplantation or computer programs for diagnosis. A proliferation of research and development has put at the doctor's disposal an endless array of drug therapies. More and more, medical science becomes medical technology as new forms of knowledge are transposed and applied, transforming the doctor into a politically powerful technologist – a technologist of the body. In order to plot the course of this radical change, and to reflect upon its limitations, we need to think through a web of ideas concerning the real nature of technology, its origins in the Greek notion of *techne*, and the connection between *techne* and *praxis*: this Gadamer does in the first essay in *The Enigma of Health*, 'Theory, technology, praxis'. Drawing upon Aristotle's account of practice in the *Nicomachean Ethics*, Gadamer shows how the 'technologization' of knowledge in the modern world distorts the traditional theory/practice relationship. For the ancient craftsman, the productive process involved the application of knowledge to a pre-planned object. The artefact emanated from the practical skill (*techne*) of the artisan. Even for Aristotle, the doctor occupied a special place because his practical skill was not directly applied to the construction of an object. Medical art produces nothing in the literal sense: health is not an object. Medicine, and this is one of the central insights Gadamer brings to an understanding of the modern world, can never be reduced to a mere skill. What the doctor seeks to bring about is health, but its return is never a direct consequence of applied skill since skilfulness only relates to the production of artefacts.

Medical practice is, if one thinks back to its primordial sense, the *art* of healing. Special consideration needs to be given to the terms 'art' and 'healing'. What the modern world is in danger of neglecting is the sense in which the real expertise of the doctor assists rather than controls the natural healing process. The doctor requires a special kind of 'phronetic' judgement (from *phronesis*, 'practical wisdom'), in aiming to restore the essential balance or equilibrium of the patient. The doctor should have no illusions that she is curing the patient with interventionary techniques. At best she can, with solicitude, tentatively apply general medical knowledge to this particular, that is, unique, individual. Medicine is both an art and a skill. The artistry displays itself as the doctor seeks to interpret the imbalance in the patient and guides the process whereby the patient recovers a lost equilibrium. Balance is required of the doctor in that she needs to make a fine discrimination between what will assist the patient and what needs to be left to the 'open domain' of nature. The illness of the patient presents the doctor with a hermeneutical problem.

So easily the doctor's intervention can be fractionally too much or too little, bringing about a complete reversal of the intended effect. Gadamer likens the doctor's art to Rilke's description of the acrobat where 'the pure too little incomprehensibly transforms itself, springs over into the empty too much'.[24] In our scientific age, Gadamer suggests, the fine discriminations of the doctor are limited because technology artificially reduces the necessity for judgement. As Gadamer says, 'the more strongly the sphere of application becomes rationalised, the more does proper exercise of judgment along with practical experience in the proper sense fail to take place' (1996, p. 17).

The true enigma of health is this. When all is said and done the doctor is not fully in control, neither is he ever in a position to completely understand the nature of health, the body, nor healing. The true concern of the practitioner is not the general nature of health but the restoration of the equilibrium of a particular, unique, individual, in his care. Ultimately health cannot be explained entirely from within the province of the scientific world. 'Illness is a social state of affairs. It is also a psychological-moral state of affairs, much more than a fact that is determinable from within the natural sciences' (1996, p. 20). More fundamental than general scientific understanding for the doctor is the range of ethical concerns relating to the care the practitioner demonstrates towards the patient and the care the patients exercise upon themselves. Dialogue, a central feature of understanding, worked out in detail in *Truth and Method*, is at the heart of the doctor/patient relationship. Through dialogue the ethical is made manifest. In discussing what has come to be known as 'medical ethics' Gadamer thankfully avoids the sterile terrain of competing and antagonistic moral principles, so often the generally accepted arena for contemporary philosophical debates, preferring the richer non-theoretical vocabulary of Aristotelian 'virtues'. The skilled practitioner is not just technically adept but possesses a repertoire of appropriate 'excellences'. A good doctor has 'bedside manner', we might say, especially if we detect trustworthiness, care, co-operation, gentle persuasion, and the like. It is in dialogue with the patient that these ethical characteristics come to the fore because only when the patient is in a position to articulate the nature of the pain, discomfort, anxiety, can the healing process begin. Good medical practice is essentially dialogical. For Gadamer, general practice is as much concerned with the 'talking cure' as more obviously language-based therapies like psychoanalysis as he argues in the last essay in the collection, 'Hermeneutics and psychiatry'.

In many ways this recent work of Gadamer echoes the writings of Michel Foucault by sharing common concerns. Foucault's analysis of the politicization and legal-medical control of the body within the knowledge/power structures of modernity (spelt out in such works as the *The Birth of the Clinic* and *Discipline and Punish*) strikes an obvious chord with Gadamer. However, Gadamer's route is not Foucault's genealogy of the bizarre and marginal. He works not at the level of discourses of power with their implicit 'hermeneutics of suspicion', but the more trusting and charitable, some would say naive, level, of the historicality of everyday language. Throughout these essays, and particularly in 'On the enigmatic character of health', Gadamer is ceaselessly vigilant to the abandoned and forgotten nuances of meaning in his reflections upon the language of health, illness and medical practice. Eschewing linguistic analysis he prefers to operate through *Destruktion*, bringing out of concealment suppressed meanings, not for the Heideggerian purpose of demonstrating the forgetfullness of metaphysics, but to highlight the ways the primeval senses of terms have been refracted or occluded in the scientific age. Part of Gadamer's purpose is to illustrate how echoes and traces of words are still – albeit in sedimented form – active and operative in the language of the present. Listening to the reverberations of more authentic meanings, a difficult but not impossible task even in our scientific age, enriches the level of reflection and understanding, making one more mindful of what has been forgotten in a culture's state of collective amnesia. A frequently used example in these essays, because it bears directly upon the medical lexicon, is the notion of 'treatment'. To emphasize the all too easily neglected interpersonal aspects of the doctor's expertise, Gadamer notes in the essay 'Philosophy and medical practice':

> The German word *Behandlung* is a rich and significant word for 'treating' people and 'handling' them with care. Within it one hears literally the word 'hand', the skilled and practised hand that can recognize problems simply through feeling and touching the affected parts of the patient's body. 'Treatment' in this sense is something which goes far beyond mere progress in modern techniques. (Gadamer, p. 99)

Common to all the essays is a dramatic motif about the limitations of technology, scientific method and their cultural influence upon medical practice in the Western world. However, it would be wrong to accuse Gadamer of a facile hostility to science, although this is a frequently heard charge against him. Gadamer's attitude to the 'scientific age' is more complicated.

The gap between the methodized world-picture and the hermeneutical openness of effective history will never be closed. The scientific project of the domination of nature, under whose shadow we cower, at least since the 'enlightenment', will never be realized. On the other hand, the increasing tension between technology and ethical life seems to be an ineradicable feature of modernity, although for Gadamer, it is a tension we can, like our own health, bring into equilibrium. He says in the Preface to *The Enigma of Health*, '[our problem] is a question of finding the right balance between our technical capacities and the need for responsible actions and choices' (Gadamer, 1996, pp. viii–ix). The anonymous medical technocrat supplants the traditional idea of the family doctor, as both friend and adviser: the patient/doctor relationship makes way for the impersonal domination of experts. Technology is taking over. Yet despite the Brave New World, we can, Gadamer suggests, reclaim the rapidly disappearing forms of collective and personal responsibility necessary to redress the balance, without fruitlessly raging against the machine. For this reason, perhaps, Gadamer is reluctant to suggest ways, through an elaborate critique of the structures of modernity, for reversing the alienating effects of change. He refrains from outlining nostrums of political resistance to the inevitable dehumanizing consequences of technology. By the 'cunning of practice' (my term, not Gadamer's), rather than Hegel's 'cunning of reason', there will always be the opportunity to move within a free space uncolonized by the ravages of strictly methodized practice. Despite pressures to the contrary, Gadamer suggests, good practice, medical or otherwise, will always have the resourcefulness or 'cunning' to prevent its total annihilation. More than this, good practice, because of its intimate connection to ethical life, depends upon social solidarity, precisely the kind of solidarity needed to develop to resist the excesses of modernity.

Is this all wishful thinking? Gadamer's level of discourse, for all its sensitivity to language, its erudition, wistful nostalgia and gently optimistic humanism, somehow fails to engage with the deafening language of market economics, perhaps the most intractable feature of modernity. The failure of most medical practitioners to extricate themselves from the baleful effects of technology is only one factor amongst many. Consideration should be given to the ideologically motivated refusal of governments to adequately fund public healthcare. Pressure of work on doctors, in under-funded clinics and hospitals, has also contributed to the problem Gadamer identifies and should be part of his diagnosis. Not withstanding these criticisms, *The Enigma of Health* is a thoroughly wise book and should be compulsory reading for anyone with a direct or passing, professional or lay, interest in medicine and healthcare. It is also an excellent introduction to the intricacies and subtleties of Gadamer's thought.

Another area of practice and a constant theme to which Gadamer returns is higher education. In the 1986 essay 'The Idea of the University',[25] echoing as it does Newman's classic defence of liberal education, Gadamer looks to the university as one place where solidarities are preserved and reconfigured. Although the modern university is as much under threat from bureaucratization as is medical practice, Gadamer sees glimmers of hope for the future. The modern institute of higher education, for all its remoteness, its destructive specialization and cosying up to big business, still offers an opportunity to discover what he calls a 'free space' which is 'not offered as a privilege to a particular class but as a human possibility which is never totally unrealized in any person and which we have been given to develop to a higher degree for everyone'.[26]

The free space seems to work in two ways. It is the opportunity for self-discovery, a space away from the regimentation of managed life enabling the possibilities of self-creation, for 'the task of our human life in general is to find free spaces and learn to move therein'.[27] The 'free space' is the place to forge new solidarities. For the university is not principally about learning, it is a place where genuine experience is encountered, 'a place where something happens to us . . . [for]. . . this small academic universe still remains one of the few precursors of the grand universe of humanity, of all human beings, who must learn to create with one another new solidarities'.[28] The university, although it is constantly under pressure from the world of business to churn out narrow specialists for the world of work, actually has the potential to be a model of a larger solidarity, a *universitas* (the whole world), where the spirit of free enquiry and the quest for a 'free space' preserves all that is necessary for the potentially dangerous open dialogue of enquiry and self-discovery.

Fanciful, over-optimistic and elitist are some of the possible charges levelled against Gadamer's utopian vision of higher education but his plea for the continued independence of mind in the *universitas scholarum*, as 'opposed to the moulding of social consciousness by the powers of the present',[29] is both timely and admirable.[30]

NOTES

1 'Solidarity' in Rorty (1989).
2 A good example is the series of interviews collected in Palmer (2001), pp. 34–5, 80–2, 85, 93, 101, 125 and 130.
3 Rorty (1989).
4 Rorty (1989), pp. 189–98.
5 Rorty (1989), p. 189.
6 Rorty (1989), p. 189.
7 Rorty (1989), p. 189.
8 Rorty (1989), p. 191.
9 Geras (1995).
10 Gadamer (2001), p. 80.
11 Rorty (1989), p. 196.
12 *Ibid.*, p. 57.
13 On this whole topic see the essay, 'Gadamer's hope' (Grondin, 2004).
14 Gadamer (2001), p. 83.
15 Gadamer (2001), p. 81.
16 Gadamer (2001), p. 82.
17 *TM*, pp. xxvii–xxxviii.
18 *TM*, p. xxviii; my italics.
19 *TM*, p. xxviii.
20 Misgeld and Nicholson (1992). The full title is *Hans-Georg Gadamer on Education, Poetry, and History: Applied Hermeneutics*.
21 Misgeld and Nicholson (1992), p. vii.
22 Misgeld and Nicholson (1992), p. 192.
23 Gadamer (1996).
24 Gadamer (1996), p. 36.
25 Gadamer, 'The idea of the university', in Misgeld and Nicholson (1992).
26 Misgeld and Nicholson, p. 56.
27 Misgeld and Nicholson, p. 59.
28 Misgeld and Nicholson, p. 59.
29 Misgeld and Nicholson, p. 57.
30 The similarities between Gadamer's conception of the university and that of his English contemporary Michael Oakeshott are uncanny. Oakeshott's writings on education are collected in Oakeshott, M., *The Voice of Liberal Learning: Michael Oakeshott on Education*. See especially the essay 'The idea of a university' (pp. 95–104).

CHAPTER 8

FELLOW TRAVELLERS AND CRITICS

GADAMER NOW

Gadamer died in 2002 at the ripe old age of 102. In some ways, by the time of his death, he was, to a younger generation of academics, something of an anachronism. Not because philosophers do not generally live into their second century, although they do not (do many of us?), but because he seemed to be the product of a vanished world lost to public memory. Sure enough, in his later years, he was fêted as the Grand Old Man of European philosophy, but there was something increasingly antiquated about his bookish defences of humanistic values in a divided, fragmented and increasingly pluralistic world, and his rather quaint respect for the power of great philosophy and literature to mould great minds and extend civilized values was out of synch with the more cynical end of century *zeitgeist*. With debates in philosophy and literary studies about gender and power politics, the elitism of canons, the effete writings of Dead White Males, Gadamer's voice seemed a little out of place, one might think. But this was not actually so because there is another story to be told. In fact Gadamer was for many one of the heroes of late twentieth-century postmodernism, or at least there is a way of reading his work as though he was a postmodernist thinker, and Gadamer was clearly aware of the sense in which his work was very close to other thinkers who questioned the central tenets of philosophical modernity and thus there is an enduring relevance of his work. Chapter 2 discussed the question of method in the context of the Enlightenment and saw Gadamer as a representative of a reaction against this philosophical movement. Such a reaction is all of a piece with postmodernism since it places the credentials of the Enlightenment in question in a similar way.

GADAMER AND POSTMODERNISM

A good deal has been written and said about postmodernism. It is a useful term, if treated with caution, as it does refer to an identifiable tendency of thought as well as a fairly specific historical period (this despite agonies about whether or not we have now reached post-postmodernism). At the risk of oversimplification postmodernism might be characterized in the following way, highlighting the convergence of its principal tenets and the key ideas of Gadamer's thought. Postmodernism is a kind of scepticism built upon a series of doubts and uneases concerning the legacy of Enlightenment thought.

Subjectivity. It is sceptical about *subjectivity*. Since Descartes, the idea of a controlling subject, an ego, an 'I', the seat of consciousness and rational reflective thought, has dominated much subsequent thought. Postmodern alternatives to this orthodox picture decentre the subject as endlessly fragmented. Gadamer's version of subjectivity is decidedly 'postmodern'; one only has to think back to the oft-quoted passage from *Truth and Method*:

> . . . [H]istory does not belong to us; we belong to it. Long before we understand ourselves through the process of self-examination, we understand ourselves in a self-evident way in the family, society, and state in which we live. The focus of subjectivity is a distorting mirror. The self-awareness of the individual is only a flickering in the closed circuits of historical life. (*TM*, p. 276)

Gadamer ridicules the idea of a controlling subject; the forces of socialization and acculturation are in play long before any move towards self-reflection is possible. And even that reflection is only a 'flickering' in the 'closed circuits of historical life', that is fitful and isolated moments of illumination and insight within the more regulating and controlling structures of language and tradition.

Anti-foundationalist. Postmodernism is sceptical about the foundations of knowledge. If the controlling subject is revealed as illusory, truth and certainty, traditionally understood, are equally shaky. The controlling subject was thought to be in direct contact with the external world but for postmodernism the subject gives way to intersubjectivity or something more ungrounded and unstable. The 'foundations' of knowledge, for Gadamer, is the network of agreements and conventions upon which language and tradition are built, and these are hardly foundations since they are constantly in a process of change.

A consequence of 'anti-foundationalism' is a deep scepticism about objective truth. Postmodernism is often characterized as embracing deep *relativism*. In denying the possibility of objective truth it asserts the relative nature of truth systems, cultures, linguistic communities. Gadamer, as we have seen, certainly wants to deny the possibility of objective truth if it means failing to acknowledge the situatedness of the subject, as it must, but, and this is a difficult one to answer, does this make Gadamer a relativist? In one sense Gadamer is a relativist about truth since he denies that propositions have a timeless quality about them; for Gadamer, as we have seen all truth is historical. But does this mean Gadamer collapses into pure subjectivity or complete arbitrariness? Nothing could be further from his own position. One of the usual consequences of radical or deep relativism is the impossibility of trans-cultural and trans-historical understanding, yet Gadamer manages to avoid this. One of the virtues of the 'fusion of horizons' is the possibility of extending one's own cultural horizon to embrace and interact with one wholly alien and remote from one's own. Because of the universality built into the hermeneutic circle (all languages, all cultures, have this much in common, they operate according to the structure of the circle), cultural relativism is avoided. Is Gadamer an ontological relativist, in other words is he relativistic about the possibility of knowing the nature of the natural non-human world? Brice Wachterhauser has put this very well when he speaks of Gadamer as a 'perspectival realist'.[1] There is a world beyond our culturally conditioned perception of it – this is the realist dimension. On the other hand we can never get a full picture of that world since interpretations constantly change, hence we can never get more than a 'perspective'. The term is deliberately mindful of 'perspectivism' the position often attributed to Friedrich Nietzsche.

Following on from relativism postmodernism is also sceptical of *science* as the dominant discourse. If truth is relative, the idea of science as a master discourse by which all other practices, activities or regional ontologies are to be judged is to be found wanting. Again, as we have already witnessed, Gadamer seems remarkably postmodern in his suspicion of all claims of science to be the master discourse, the version of knowledge by which all other versions are to be assessed. And finally, because there is no master discourse there is a postmodern scepticism about the *traditional separation of*

philosophy and literature. There is nothing, for the postmodern theorist, essential to philosophy or literature; they are both just kinds
of writing. So for postmodernism the traditional border dispute
between philosophy and literature is just much ado about nothing.
In a very sketchy way we see the rudiments of the postmodern position and we also see why it is so easy to put Gadamer up there
amongst the heroes of postmodernity.

FELLOW TRAVELLERS: WITTGENSTEIN AND RORTY

Few contemporary thinkers have acknowledged a direct influence
from Gadamer's philosophical hermeneutics, although many have
indirectly absorbed his ideas.[2] It is worth mentioning two important philosophers whose work massively overlaps with that of
Gadamer, even though neither would declare themselves as herm-
eneuticists or postmodernists.[3] The thinkers I have in mind are
Ludwig Wittgenstein and Richard Rorty.

The similarities between Gadamer and Wittgenstein are very
striking. Until recently the similarities between Gadamer and
Wittgenstein have largely passed unnoticed. I have sought to rectify
this in my own writings.[4] Although they share much in common
I suggest in this work that Wittgenstein's later conception of language
is limited by its failure to take a 'hermeneutical turn'. Wittgenstein's
conception of linguistic rules lacks the kind of flexibility encounted
in philosophical hermeneutics. Consequently Wittgenstein is unable
to show how the language-games of the present link up to those of the
past. Neither is he able to account for the creative resources in linguistic usage, so evident in Gadamer's hermeneutics. First and foremost they are undeniably what I have termed 'anti-foundationalist'
thinkers. For Gadamer there is no solid matrix, either in reason or
experience, upon which the knowing subject can ground knowledge.
This is precisely the sort of position Wittgenstein affirms in
Philosophical Investigations and *On Certainty*. Wittgenstein's 'private
language argument' is designed to show how language is essentially a
public matter. Meanings are not derived from the inner resources
of the individual speaker but the complex network of overlapping
'language-games'. Language is not grounded in its power to represent
or name individual experience; its force comes from the public agreements, conventions and censuses, which constitute the language-
games. In a sense the language-games are arbitrary as they are

without the kind of solid foundations Cartesians and empiricists would deem necessary. Gadamer's dialogical account of language is very close to Wittgenstein. In fact although Gadamer does not speak of 'language-games' he does, as we have already noted in relation to aesthetics, bring out the playful element within language. And the play is not just to illustrate the sense in which meanings are constantly in the process of creation and re-creation; it shows how meanings are beyond the control of the individual linguistic players. Once again we see a similarity with Wittgenstein. The 'language-game' is devised to show how language is essentially practical – just as there is no game without people to play it there can be no language without people to speak it and use it. In the case of both Gadamer and Wittgenstein there can be no real making sense of language from a theoretical perspective, no philosophy of language; language is essentially a practical activity, and can never be made an object of quasi-scientific investigation. For both Gadamer and Wittgenstein everyday language is in order as it is. The suggestion, from some philosophers, that language needs to be reformed and radically overhauled or turned into a more technical and precise means of communication is far from the thoughts of Gadamer and the later Wittgenstein. Both thinkers are aware of the possible traps language might set for the unwary; becoming ensnared in dangerous metaphysics is something to which they are both alert.

> When philosophers use a word – 'knowledge', 'being', 'object', 'I', 'proposition', 'name' – and try to grasp the *essence* of the thing, one must always ask oneself: is the word ever actually used in this way in the language which is its original home? What *we* do is to bring words back from their metaphysical to their everyday use.[5]

Despite the dangerous temptation to use language in the service of metaphysics, Wittgenstein reminds us that language is first and foremost the language of the everyday, untainted by metaphysical aberrations. Gadamer echoes this sentiment when he distances himself from Heidegger. Heidegger spoke of the 'language of metaphysics' and how it had found its way into all forms of speech. Against this Gadamer offers the following Wittgensteinian thought:

> Is it the language of metaphysics alone that achieves this continual coming-to-language of our Being-in-the-world? Certainly it is the

language of metaphysics, but further behind it is the language of the Indo-Germanic peoples, which makes such thinking capable of being formulated. But can a language – or a family of languages – ever properly be called the language of metaphysical thinking, just because metaphysics was thought, or what would be more, anticipated in it? Is not language always the language of the homeland and the process of becoming-at-home in the world?[6]

In other ways also the similarities are remarkable. Both adopt a deep suspicion of scientism and the need to see all achievements in terms of scientific respectability. And they share a common suspicion of technology and the general capacity of modernity to overshadow deeper truths. But Wittgenstein is not Gadamer. There are differences in style and substance. Firstly, let us deal with the matter of style. Increasingly, in Wittgenstein's later work his style is fragmentary and aphoristic. This is in part to do with his way of working, that is, the short descriptive account of the ways a certain word, concept or phrase is used in everyday language. It also has to do with his desire to highlight the particularity of things, the need to keep away from that malignant philosophical urge he terms a 'craving for generality'. Gadamer on the other hand is more traditional and less experimental in his writing. At the same time we might say his style reflects his thought; for Gadamer the stress is not upon the unique and the particular but what it is that we, as language-users, actually share and have in common. For Gadamer, there is in the modern age too much stress upon difference and not enough attention to what in fact binds us as a species, what we share in common.[7]

Richard Rorty, like Wittgenstein, is often proclaimed an anti-foundationalist and postmodern thinker, and his version of pragmatism frequently overlaps with philosophical hermeneutics. Anti-foundationalism is important as an idea to bring our two thinkers together. Rorty's version is spelt out in his ground-breaking work *Philosophy and the Mirror of Nature*. His principal claim is that Western philosophy, since the birth of philosophical modernism, is in the grip of a powerful myth about the nature of truth. Human truth is taken to be a reflection, a mirror image of the way things are, and philosophy is locked into this idea of truth as an accurate representing relationship between the perceiver and the objects of perception.

Against this, Rorty speaks of the need to break the spell of this metaphor by finding new ways of talking, new alternative narratives for re-imagining truth. Rorty's procedure is historical; his thesis depends upon looking through the history of the development of modern philosophical thought to see that this metaphor of the 'mirror of nature' is a constantly recurring one. Rorty's rejection of an orthodox account of truth is important and far reaching but his procedure, to approach the question historically, is ground-breaking because it came at a time in the development of analytic philosophy when philosophers were largely oblivious to historical considerations. As we have already noted, this procedure is all of a piece with the one adopted by Gadamer. The whole of *Truth and Method* is an engagement with the history of philosophy.

In the concluding part of *Philosophy and the Mirror of Nature* Rorty turns to hermeneutics, specifically the philosophical hermeneutics of Gadamer,[8] to suggest an alternative to representation. It is to Gadamer's conception of philosophy as dialogue and conversation that Rorty turns for a more dialogical and hermeneutical model for truth. In his subsequent writings the themes of conversation and dialogue have become even more important ideas in Rorty's attack upon orthodox accounts of language and truth and his closeness to Gadamer is evident.[9] The idea of solidarity assumed increasing importance in the later work of Gadamer and in similar fashion it became more important in Rorty's quest for a mirrorless ethics and politics. What Rorty finds in Gadamer is the emphasis upon truth as dialogue. Against the idea of truth as representation is the thought that truth, if it is anything, is edification, providing new ways of speaking, made possible by dialogue and conversation. Rorty's celebrated move to edification owes much to the work of Gadamer. Rorty says:

> Since 'education' sounds a bit flat, and *Bildung* a bit too foreign, I shall use 'edification' to stand for this project of finding new, better, more interesting, more fruitful ways of speaking. The attempt to edify (ourselves and others) may consist in the hermeneutic activity of making connections between our own culture and some exotic culture or historical period, or between our own discipline and another discipline which seems to pursue incommensurable aims in an incommensurable vocabulary. (1980, p. 360)

Rorty's 'edification' is approximate to Gadamer's 'understanding'; both imagine ways of building bridges between unfamiliar cultures and language-games through hermeneutic dialogue and conversation. As I sought to show in the last chapter, despite the proximity between Gadamer and Rorty there is plenty to divide them. I suggested earlier that Rorty's contingency, from which all elements of social life appear to spring, is far less grounded and arbitrary than Gadamer's tradition and hence lacks plausibility. Languages and traditions are constantly changing and are clearly not guided by a *telos* or a world-historical narrative, but they stand as powerful influences with cultural life – more powerful than Rorty appears to admit.

GADAMER'S CRITICS

Philosophical hermeneutics has always had its critics, unsettling the left and the right, the philosophical avant-garde and the traditionalists. E. D. Hirsch, the American literary critic, one of the first English-language commentators on Gadamer,[10] took issue with what he took to be the indeterminacy of meaning evident in *Truth and Method*. For Hirsch, Gadamer radically destabilizes meaning to such an extent that language loses any sense of permanence and stability. What fixes meaning, according to Hirsch, is authorial intention. Even with the early hermeneutics of Schleiermacher, the author has no privileged access to the meaning of a word or a text; in fact the point of hermeneutics is to understand the text better than the author did. Even Lewis Carroll was able to satirize this position when Humpty Dumpty is made to declare his intention to make words mean whatever he wants them to mean. For Hirsch, meaning is fixed by authorial meaning and he rejects Gadamer's putative relativization and destabilization of meaning. Part of Hirsch's criticism of Gadamer turns on the difference between the *meaning* of a word or a text and its *significance*. Gadamer is assumed to conflate the two and use them interchangeably. For Hirsch, the meaning of a text, in particular, is fixed by the author's intention; the text is what the author says it is. Hence, the meaning is unchanging and the point of interpretation and criticism is to uncover or reveal the author's meaning. The meaning of a great work of literature does not change over time and thus reconstruction of the author's intentions opens up the real meaning of a text.

When Gadamer speaks of the meaning of a text, according to Hirsch he is actually mistaken and is really referring to the text's *significance*, which does, he agrees, change over time. For example,

Shakespearean drama appears to have had little significance for the culture of the nineteenth century despite its immense popularity in its own day and its revival in the early part of the twentieth century. The fortunes of texts rise and fall with fashion or the spirit of the age and thus it makes sense to talk of the changing significance of a text, *for a particular era*, but not a change in meaning.

Curiously enough, despite radically different conceptions of textual meaning both Gadamer and Hirsch support the idea of a canon of great literature. In the case of Hirsch, well after his critique of Gadamer, he pioneered the idea of 'cultural literacy', advocating the drawing up of a checklist of great ideas and authors and works of which every educated citizen (American citizen) should be aware. But whereas Hirsch's literary canon is a repository of relatively unchanging civilizing ideas and concepts, Gadamer's canon is ceaselessly in a process of redefinition. Gadamer's canon, as a partner in dialogue, is constantly changing. Gadamer's canon is made up of texts, the voices of which draw the reader into conversation. This idea of the horizon of the text addressing the reader makes good sense. It explains actually why certain books are in the canon and why certain others are not; it is their power to address those in search of understanding, which is, ultimately, self-understanding. Texts that address us in the present may not have addressed those in the past. For example, the rediscovery of forgotten, banished or lost texts by emancipated and freethinking women of the past, the drawing of such texts into the newly defined canon, newly defined by feminist audiences, seem to be examples of the way texts from the past can be re-invigorated and revived. Every text will, at some point in its interpretive history, address an audience: even if it goes unheard for a time it will at some stage meet the needs and questions of future generations. In many senses texts can be well ahead of their time: only once they draw us into their horizon do we start to engage with them. Gadamer's canon is not a frozen monument to the past but an ever-changing, living voice in the ceaseless conversation of humanity.

Jürgen Habermas and the left critique of Gadamer follow a different trajectory. Habermas sees virtue in Gadamer's revival of hermeneutics; it represents a valuable and timely alternative to positivism in the social sciences. Nevertheless, Habermas seeks to unleash philosophical hermeneutics from its conservative defence of the *status quo* and its failure to adopt a critical stance towards tradition. Much of the debate with Habermas[11] turns on different understandings of 'reason' and 'dialogue'. In simple terms, Habermas is characterized as a defender of the Enlightenment project, and an upholder of its political agenda of freedom and emancipation. What use is knowledge if we cannot use it to make the world a better place and free ourselves from the constraints the Enlightenment deemed oppressive? Habermas defends a version of reason, universal reason through which debates and rival positions might be tested. But has Gadamer abolished the idea of universal rationality since he has made reason a function of dialogue, each mode of speech and dialogue assuming its own canons of reason? As well as defending a traditional account of reason, Habermas wants to use it in the service of dialogue.

Gadamer, it is argued, fails to account for the possibility of dialogue being deformed and distorted. According to the Gadamerian picture, transparent and unimpeded communication is always an option; dialogue is as much about negotiation as it is articulation and some measure of understanding is always possible, no matter what divisions initially exist. The 'fusion of horizons' ensures that some measure of clarity of understanding is always under way if never finally concluded. Gadamer speaks of a necessary *trust* in communication, a trust in the willingness of the other in dialogue to reach out, in good faith, to reach understanding. Without the assumption of that trust language would constantly break down lacking the necessary flexibility within which trust operates. Gadamer expressed this well when he commented: 'Social life depends on our acceptance of everyday speech as trustworthy. We cannot order a taxi without this trust. Thus understanding is the average case not misunderstanding.'[12] Against the 'hermeneutics of trust' Gadamer demonstrates here, one might oppose it with what Paul Ricoeur has aptly termed a 'hermeneutics of suspicion'. With the latter there is a manifest distrust about the transparency of communication. Could it not be the case, one might argue, that everyday language is systematically distorted? Distorted by the unperceived force of ideology or the structures of power, class, gender or the unconscious? Gadamer's trust in the possibility of unclouded and direct communication could seem naïve in the face of the various deformations to which language-users may be subjected. In class-divided cultures it is the unwitting force of ideology that Gadamer's naïve hermeneutics appears to be unaware, opponents could argue. Habermas wants what Gadamer wants, namely, edifying forms of dialogue, but what he terms 'unconstrained dialogue' is only possible once the structures of ideology have been rooted out by the power of reason. Gadamer is deeply suspicious of such trust in the power of a universalized reason, to which his rehabilitation of prejudice bears witness. Gadamer finds the idea of liberation from the constraining power of dialogue to be misplaced. Dialogue is not to be subsumed under some metric of rationality; it will always betray evidence of persuasive and rhetorical forms of speech pulling against the desire to impose something like rational reflection upon articulations.

Gadamer comments: 'I find it frighteningly unreal when people like Habermas ascribe to rhetoric a compulsory quality that one must reject in favour of unconstrained, rational dialogue' (*TM*, p. 568). Habermas's Enlightenment-inspired trust in the power to be extricated from oppressive ideological forms of speech in the interests of political emancipation is doubtful from the point of view of philosophical hermeneutics. For Gadamer, rhetoric is part of the make-up of the language of everyday speech and the idea that we could escape it in the interests of avoiding baleful social manipulation is as fanciful as the attempt to make the constitutive prejudices of consciousness an object of rational enquiry. Despite the evident ideological distortions of communication and despite the powers of rhetorical persuasion ordinary language is given to, for Gadamer philosophical hermeneutics offers adequate resources to meet such challenges.

Other challenges from the political left question Gadamer's seemingly irrational dependence upon the idea of tradition. Surely one needs to take account of the traditions of resistance and subversion of the hegemonic tradition, those suspicious of an overarching tradition might argue? Gadamer's version of tradition seems to be an all-pervasive force within which all forms of language, history and culture are subsumed. His conception of tradition is of one homogenous power and he neglects the point that within traditions there are in fact counter-traditions, and, as Michel Foucault has demonstrated, traditions of subversion. Once again this kind of position takes its cue from Enlightenment thought, perceiving all mention of tradition as oppressive and untested by the lights of reason.

Many have challenged Gadamer on this very point. If all is part of a unitary tradition, is there ever a point outside the tradition for radical, critical reflection and the power to initiate change? Is Gadamer forced into a position whereby criticism, necessarily outside the circuits of tradition, in the name of common humanity, universality, is impossible? Put another way: is Gadamer's hermeneutics ultimately no more than a bolster and defence of the *status quo* and hence deep political conservativism? Terry Eagleton, the Marxist literary theorist, criticizes Gadamer along the following lines:

> History, for Gadamer, is not a place of struggle, discontinuity and exclusion but a 'continuing chain', an ever-flowing river, almost, one might say, a club of the like-minded. Historical differences are tolerantly conceded, but only because they are effectively liquidated by an understanding which 'bridg(es) the temporal distance which separates the interpreter from the text'.[13]

Eagleton's idea that Gadamer sees all conflict as smoothed over by the 'ever-flowing river' of tradition links up with the above criticism of an absence of the resources for critique in philosophical hermeneutics. Eagleton continues, 'Tradition holds an authority to which we must submit: there is little possibility of critically challenging that authority, and no speculation that its influence may be anything but benevolent.'[14] Conceding everything to tradition, submitting to given (political and other) authorities is clearly, for Eagleton, a mark of a deeply conservative politics conjuring up a frightening power exerted by the past upon the present and the future, reminiscent of Marx's wonderful one-liner: 'The tradition of all the dead generations weighs like a nightmare on the brain of the living.'

As Chapter 3 emphasized, this Enlightenment-inspired version of tradition is a far cry from Gadamer's. Eagleton's Marxist idea of history as struggle emphasizes a constant oppositional movement. Gadamer does not speak of struggle but the dynamic within hermeneutics represents a constant motion, as exemplified in the notion of play. Admittedly, it is, in conversation and dialogue, a move towards reconciliation and compromise, but, and this is the point, full resolution is never achieved. Gadamer's tradition is not the nightmarish weight of dead generations but a ceaseless dialogical interaction between past and present. But intrinsic to the dialogue are differing viewpoints. The images of the 'continuing chain' and the 'ever-flowing river' are inappropriate if they are meant to suggest a seamless harmony.

But is Eagleton right to portray Gadamer as a conservative in the overtly political sense? In conversations about his political allegiances Gadamer constantly denies either that he had any truck with the ideas of National Socialism – as we have already discussed in

Chapter 1 – or that he was even a conservative.[15] This, despite the reception of philosophical hermeneutics as a defence of tradition and a theoretical justification of reactionary politics. On the contrary, Gadamer speaks of himself as a political liberal and there is much in his theoretical writings to reinforce this self-image. There is a deep parallel between Gadamer's conception of dialogue and the central commitments enshrined in liberalism.

Consider the Gadamerian conception of dialogue. As already established, dialogue, at the heart of hermeneutics, is in philosophical terms, an admission that no individual or community has privileged access to truth, truth being provisional, fallible and many-sided. Following from this there is always the chance that the other (that is another in dialogue) can expose a weakness in a position. Truth is dialogue. On reflection Gadamer's conception of the fallibility of truth looks very like the brand of liberalism outlined by John Stuart Mill in his classic defence, *On Liberty*. For Mill, vigorous public debate is at the heart of politics. No one position can automatically assume orthodoxy; even democracy has to be argued for and defended. For this reason, no political commitment, no matter how strongly believed, can avoid the necessity to be tested, discussed and open to critical scrutiny – even ridicule – in an open forum. The fallibility in all perspectives, including strongly held political beliefs, means they can never be taken for granted, never permitted to ossify into received wisdom, the party line, or unchallenged dogma. For Mill, dogma is the fate of any political position society no longer feels the need to debate or discuss. It is held onto as an incontrovertible article of faith. I am suggesting that there are many parallels between Mill's liberalism and the implicit liberalism in Gadamer's hermeneutics. Gadamer too stresses fallibility in human affairs and the dialogical nature of understanding as a way of mediating between differing, even opposing political creeds. And he also implies a politics of compromise, finding the middle way, listening to the voice of the other. In reflecting on the various peace processes, in Israel and Ireland, and throughout the world, there is the language of compromise and the need for resolving conflict through dialogue and seeing things from the point of view of an opposing community. With these in mind, we see even more starkly the way a hermeneutical politics of dialogue is constantly aspired to if not actually achieved. I have only hinted at it here, but what is suggested is that there is a practical politics that emerges from philosophical hermeneutics and this is remarkably like the classical liberalism of Mill and not the reactionary conservativism all too frequently attributed to Gadamer. And his is a democratic and egalitarian politics dependent upon the participation of all voices – individual not representative voices – in the dialogue. Grand political abstractions have no place in a hermeneutical politics.

Just as one has to tease a politics out of Gadamer's work (because he seldom explicitly thematizes one),[16] it is possible to relate hermeneutics to the realm of practical ethics. Like the hermeneutical politics outlined above there is the germ of a similar ethics to be constructed along the same lines. Dialogue is the structure of hermeneutical understanding; it also provides the basis for a practical ethics. True dialogue, by its very nature, demands patient listening to the voice of the other, discretion, courtesy, and again, like the political virtues above, a recognition that no one voice has sole authority or a monopoly on truth. So it can be argued that an ethics – where the hermeneutical circle is already implicit – becomes more evident when the implicit is made explicit and those particular virtues of patience, discretion, discernment and empathy – actually classic moral virtues – are brought to the fore. Along with virtue ethics, Gadamer is singularly wary of grand ethical theory dependent as it is upon abstract principles. Just as virtue ethics takes its cue from Aristotle so too does Gadamer's version. In *Truth and Method* there is a detailed section on 'The hermeneutic relevance of Aristotle'.[17] Gadamer finds in Aristotle not a fully fledged hermeneutics but a version of the hermeneutic circle relevant to his own position.

Techne with regard to production and *phronesis* (prudence or practical wisdom) with regard to action are part of Aristotle's taxonomy of practical states of mind. *Techne*, although described by Aristotle as a 'state by virtue of which the soul possesses truth', is clearly not the state of knowing appropriate for action because the end of *techne* is production unlike other states of knowing where the object is an activity. Technical knowledge presupposes the application of rules and techniques with the object of creating something, a clear conception of which is grasped beforehand. Preceding the act of production the agent possesses both knowledge of what is to be made and a firm grasp of the guiding principles and rules to which the object will conform. Success in production is determined by conformity of the procedures to the object.

Concerning moral action there are neither hard and fast principles to be drawn upon nor an object to which knowledge should be directed. The good person knows she has to act or refrain from acting in a certain way but never reflects in advance upon the appropriate response. Technical knowledge is always for the sake of something else; not so with action. The quality possessed by the good person is *phronesis*, a 'reasoned state or capacity' (Aristotle), or an intuition, about the appropriate action to perform (in the light of more general knowledge about the constituents of a good life). The knowledge required for action is intrinsically related to the self-conceptions of the agent and cannot be codified or formulated in terms of principles, nor can it be reduced to a reliable method and be taught. The good person is one disposed to act out of habituation.

Becoming good is a relatively unreflective matter. Habits of character are picked up by following the example of those already in possession of virtue. We are drawn into the moral tradition of desirable actions, generous acts, truthful acts, and so forth, but the accumulated habits will not offer guidance as to whether in this particular situation one must choose X or Y. Each situation is utterly unique: its strangeness exposes the inadequacy of general rules. Rules by their very nature can never be programmatically applied to specific cases.

The hermeneutical dimension to *phronesis* is now explicit in the problem of application. In performing an action I apply the generality of what I have learnt in the past – via the tradition – to the specificity of the potential course of action in the present. *Phronesis* reveals the real structure of understanding; not as a knowing subject grasping an object but as an experience through which the prejudices or habits, passed on in the tradition, encounter the strange and the new. The novelty is not tamed by being classified according to some organizing principle; on the contrary, it is disruptively experience as it pulls us up short. For example, in deciding what to do, either X or Y, I have no way of knowing whether X or Y are genuinely classifiable as instances of general rules. The habits of everyday morality inform me that I must not lie but is what I am doing *now* lying, or is it something else? And what I am doing *now* is not identical to anything I have ever done before however similar. This is the sense in which every situation is experienced as both novel and unique. But for all these problems the person of *phronesis* will know how to proceed since customs and habits by their nature are both flexible and adaptable. On the other hand, explicit rules do not allow for any measure of interpretive negotiation being intrinsically rigid.

DECONSTRUCTIVE CRITICISM

Terry Eagleton's critical comments on philosophical hermeneutics, in the previous section, have implications far wider than politics. He speaks of how 'historical differences are tolerantly conceded, but only because they are effectively liquidated by an understanding which "bridg(es) the temporal distance which separates the interpreter from the text"'. There are no enduring differences on this interpretation of Gadamer because they will always be defused by tradition. This raises an important question occupying so much theoretical debate since Derrida and Levinas, concerning the nature of otherness, difference or alterity. In abstract terms, the question is this, is it possible or desirable to keep the other Other, or must the other always collapse into some version of the same? In some ways this is as much a political as it is a philosophical question. If the Other is taken to be someone outside a specific community, various difficult questions need to be confronted. Should the Other be respected in their otherness or should one reach out and seek some kind of identity, a common humanity, for example. These questions are potentially political because the other could be seen as a member of another gender, another culture, or even simply as another person.

At some grand philosophical level the question of Otherness really emerges from Hegelian philosophy. Hegel's philosophy is about the journey of *Geist* (or Spirit) through world history. Spirit can be interpreted as either God or reason and the point, for Hegel, is to demonstrate that the development of world history is at the same time the development of Spirit coming to know itself. The detail of Hegel's argument is incredibly complicated but in essence he reveals that Spirit comes to know itself as spirit in the course of its own historical development. Whatever divisions first appear in history are seen as stages of the development of Spirit. In other words, there is no real sense of difference or alterity in Hegel's philosophical system, because everything reveals itself to be spirit in some particular mode or appearance. If one were to replace spirit with tradition, the criticism Eagleton makes about Gadamer's denial of historical difference makes a little more sense. The question then arises, does Gadamer collapse everything into tradition in just the same way as many claim Hegel collapses everything into Spirit? If he does, then the endless hermeneutical play of interpretation, and the ceaseless dialogue of understanding that is always seemingly under way but never finally concluded and resolved, is merely window-dressing for a triumphant tradition into which all elements of discord can eventually be cashed. But this flies in the face of the ever-moving, unresolved tradition in Gadamer. And as he suggests in the concluding section of *Truth and Method* the hermeneutical is not unlike the dialectical. Behind Eagleton's version of history as struggle lies the standard Marxist notion of the dialectic, whereby the dynamo of change is a process of contradiction and negation. This process is not unlike the hermeneutical tension between parts and whole and does, in effect, allow for the possibility of the struggle or difference philosophical hermeneutics, it is often claimed, forecloses. Whereas Gadamer stresses dialogue as the vehicle for the movement of thought in language he is aware of the possible criticism of the Hegelian position. 'Hegel's dialectic is a monologue of thinking', he asserts, for it 'tries to carry out in advance what matures little by little in every genuine conversation' (*TM*, p. 369). This demonstrates the 'tension-filled proximity' Gadamer speaks of, describing his relation to Hegel; a certain closeness but one not without problems. He rejects the Hegelian monologue of Spirit articulating itself, but affirms the idea of the enrichment of tradition in the ceaseless conversation. Gadamer refers to himself as 'an advocate of the "bad infinite" for which the end keeps on delaying its arrival' (Gadamer, 1981, p. 40). By this he means that he rejects the Hegelian idea of a *telos* and a *terminus ad quem* to history: there is no endpoint to tradition where all is resolved and alienations overcome; on the contrary, 'the conversation that we are' is interminable.

Following a similar line of enquiry to the above but from a less explicitly political stance is the critique of philosophical hermeneutics advanced by Jacques Derrida. In Paris in 1981 Gadamer and Derrida were brought together in a meeting that was obviously billed as a confrontation between hermeneutics and deconstruction. Gadamer, mindful of Derrida's presence, presented a paper entitled 'Text and interpretation' which was directed towards an explanation of his hermeneutics in relation to, and more to the point, an accommodation of, deconstruction.[18] The paper is not only a precise and condensed account of philosophical hermeneutics but also demonstrates the generosity of Gadamer's position for he, consistent with the assumption that dialogue is always possible whatever the measure of disagreement and incomprehension, continuously searches for a common ground with deconstruction.

Derrida's response to the scholarly presentation of Gadamer is brief and enigmatic. The basis of his reply focuses on a passing reference Gadamer makes to the 'good will' he claims inevitably accompanies understanding. This is a reasonably familiar idea; understanding requires a degree of reaching out to make sense of what the other is seeking to say. Also known as the 'principle of charity' in the analytical tradition, it is a recognition that language is riddled with ambiguities and understanding requires a charitable assumption that what is being said is intelligible and the listener or reader gives the benefit of the doubt, as it were, and responds with a sympathetic ear. For Gadamer, language operates on the assumption that within it one both seeks to understand and be understood. Derrida homes in on the reference to 'good will' and sees in it the trace of the old metaphysics. The suggestion is first that Gadamer affirms some kind of Kantian idea of 'good will' and that this is further distorted in what Derrida terms a 'good will to power' with the suggestion that hermeneutics has learnt nothing from the Nietzschean – and deconstructive – suspicions about deferred and disseminated meanings. At issue for Derrida is the workability or otherwise of the fusion of horizons. Gadamer's hermeneutical claim is that mutual understanding is possible because the context of meaning, the horizon, can be expanded to include another horizon. In speaking of 'good will' it can be made to appear – without the principle of charity or good will! – as though this all depends upon a metaphysical act of will. Understanding a form of words is possible, on Gadamer's account, because negotiation permits a measure of agreement and linguistic meaning is, at bottom, agreement. But how does one know when agreement has been reached and there is a mutuality of horizons to speak of commonality? For Derrida, the kind of agreement hermeneutics presupposes needs to give way to indeterminacy and difference. 'Understanding is always understanding-differently',[19] Gadamer proclaims, seeking to show that his position is actually very close to deconstruction. If meaning for deconstruction is always the result of breaches, disruptions and disseminations, it is not that far removed from Gadamer's assertions that 'understanding is always understanding differently'. Here also there is no fixed and final meaning – it is always under way, constantly modified in the process of interpretation.

NOTES

1 See B. R. Wachterhauser, 'Gadamer's realism: The "belongingness" of word and reality', pp. 148–71, in Wachterhauser (1994).
2 In the Anglo-Saxon philosophical tradition Gadamer's work has clearly made its mark upon John McDowell and Donald Davidson. In the continental tradition one thinks of Jürgen Habermas, Gianni Vattimo and Paul Ricoeur, whose work, despite points of difference, owe much of their inspiration to Gadamer.
3 Although Wittgenstein died long before the term 'postmodernism' came on the scene he is frequently proclaimed as one its founding fathers and his influence is apparent.
4 Lawn (2004).
5 Wittgenstein (2001), § 118.
6 Gadamer (1994), p. 78.
7 Some have suggested that actually Wittgenstein was attempting the same kind of position when he speaks of the natural history of the species. See the section 'Wittgenstein's naturalism' in Lawn (2004), pp. 199–223.
8 See Rorty (1980), especially p. 357–64.
9 At Gadamer's 100th birthday celebration Richard Rorty, amongst many of the other of the world's leading philosophers, was present. His encomium was printed in the *London Review of Books* (Rorty, 2000).
10 See E. D. Hirsch's essay 'Gadamer's theory of interpretation', an appendix to his *Validity in Interpretation* (1967).
11 For details of Gadamer's debate with Habermas see Chapters 9 and 10 of *The Hermeneutics Reader* (Mueller-Vollmer, 1986).
12 Misgeld and Nicholson (1992), p. 71.
13 Eagleton (1983), p. 73.
14 Eagleton (1983), p. 73.
15 Cf Rée (1995). In an interview in *Radical Philosophy* Gadamer is drawn on his postwar political allegiances. Gadamer lived through the period of student unrest in Europe and the US but by the time of the late 1960s he was already retired from full-time professional life and he seems to have been relatively untroubled by the activities of the student movement.
16 In the interviews in later life Gadamer's political allegiances are quite evident. See the section on 'Practical philosophy', Gadamer (2001), pp. 78–85.
17 *TM*, pp. 312–24.
18 The contributions of both Gadamer and Derrida at the meeting in Paris, along with a collection of essays commenting upon the meeting, are collected in Michelfelder and Palmer (1989).
19 Michelfelder and Palmer (1989), p. 96.

CONCLUSION

The following piece of verse is the epigraph at the beginning of *Truth and Method*:

> Catch only what you've thrown yourself, all is
> mere skill and little gain;
> but when you're suddenly the catcher of a ball
> thrown by an eternal partner
> with accurate and measured swing
> towards you, to your center, in an arch
> from the great bridgebuilding of God:
> why catching then becomes a power –
> not yours, a world's.
>
> (From Rainer Maria Rilke's *Sonnets for Orpheus*)

On the face of it, the sonnet's message is theological, easily taken to be a metaphor for divine revelation or man's relationship to God. However, on closer examination the meaning of the poem proves to be more elusive and open to many interpretations, in a manner not unlike philosophical hermeneutics with its notion of language as constantly surpassing particular interpretations. What is so apposite about the use of this extract from Rilke is its remarkable ability to evoke a host of Gadamerian themes in *Truth and Method*. The throwing of the ball in a game is reminiscent of the stress Gadamer places upon play as that constant movement between art work and viewer and the character of play in language where the words are always greater than the speaker, just as the team is always greater than the individual player. And the poem suggests a dialogue, one so powerful as to conjure up a whole world, indicative of language's ability to open up the human, social, sphere of tradition. And there is the mention of 'bridgebuilding', evoking the potential within language to reach out and fuse horizons. Despite an individual's constraint within a specific language, culture and world-view, there is always the possibility of trans-cultural understanding, of seeking both to understand and be understood. If the hermeneutical movement is genuinely universal, as Gadamer suggests, then some kind of negotiation and accommodation between languages and cultures (the 'eternal partner'?) is always possible. And just as the accommodation that makes understanding viable, within a specific culture, is ephemeral and provisional, so too is that between cultures. In other words, the forms of interpretive understanding that are required for communication to be possible across one culture are the same between cultures. This is a debatable point but philosophical hermeneutics makes a plausible case for trans-cultural understanding.

Rilke's 'bridgebuilding' is at the core of philosophical hermeneutics. A bridge between the past and the present is made possible by the notion of tradition, stretching as it does from the cultures and languages of the past to those of the present. The dialogue between past and present is not unproblematic but limited forms of understanding are always present even if they are, at the same time, constantly under way and inconclusive. Bridges are invariably crossed between the present and the future. Gadamer is not a conservative defender of the *status quo* as suggested by many of his critics; his hermeneutics has enough critical edge to reject the conditions of the present and envisage alternative futures. The theme in his later work of extended solidarities, within applied hermeneutics, is clearly presented as a buffer against the excesses of instrumental reasoning, technology and the decline of the public sphere – themes common to critical theory and advanced by Gadamer. And in some of the later works, he speaks approvingly of the need for utopias[1] and a secular hope for a better world.

In the realm of more theoretical philosophy it is possible to imagine other forms of bridgebuilding. We have already acknowledged the deep rift within academic philosophy, that is, the division between analytic and continental philosophy. Philosophical hermeneutics, despite its continental lineage, is generally blind to the warring factions within philosophy and could be used as a model for bringing together the two traditions.[2] The emphasis upon dialogue in philosophical hermeneutics presents itself as a model of good practice and this in itself could encourage a greater spirit of co-operation between mutually hostile factions. To advocate dialogue is at the same time to promote negotiation and to present an image of philosophy as best conducted in a spirit of humility and genuine searching. Since no one individual or school of thought has any greater access to truth than any other, the spirit of co-operation and collective enquiry, in the manner Socrates sought to cultivate in the Platonic dialogues, is evident within philosophical hermeneutics. The corollary to dialogue and the spirit of negotiation is a criticism of the more monological, and self-referential style and approach to philosophy. The gladiatorial and combative point-scoring from those whose interest is more in winning arguments than in making tentative steps towards a shared truth could learn much from Gadamer.

There is also a tendency in much contemporary philosophy to find oneself within a narrow specialism and unable to seek out the bigger picture, unable to see how 'things hang together', as Richard Rorty puts it, quoting Sellars. It seems Gadamer has something to tell us about this topic. If one were to ask how Gadamer's philosophical position is to be characterized, in conventional terms, it is difficult to know how to respond. He is not doing metaphysics, epistemology, philosophy of language, and the other discretely packaged traditional subjects within the discipline. Nor is he a systematic philosopher, like Hegel, capable of showing how these subjects all hang together within a vast system. What Gadamer offers is something between the two. Hermeneutics is relevant and applicable to all areas of philosophy and is able to provide an overview that the narrow specialism lacks. In fact what Gadamer offers in his work is very like that most ancient of qualities, wisdom. This is something the modern world appears to have lost sight of, partly as a result of regionalizing knowledge and neglecting the ways it is interconnected and linked. In fact the modern world sees itself as predicated upon knowledge. One hears much about the 'knowledge society' and the importance of knowledge. Even philosophy, as part of its modernist legacy, dwells upon 'theory of knowledge' as though it is the kernel of its enterprise. So what happened to wisdom? Gadamer, drawing upon the Aristotelian concept of *phronesis* or 'practical wisdom', as he does in much of his work, reinstates wisdom and looks to philosophical hermeneutics for that general understanding that brings things together and gives genuine insight.

Gadamer's work, with its emphasis upon language, should be appealing to analytic philosophers. The omnipresence of 'linguisticality' and the need to focus upon the minute changes in meaning over time are fundamental to the project of philosophical hermeneutics and could make common concern with the interest in language in analytic philosophy. Gadamer's suspicion of metaphysics and his willingness to stay within the confines of ordinary language, the language of the 'homeland' as he terms it, once again chimes in with the assumptions and procedures of much analytic philosophy. Philosophical hermeneutics has the advantage of distancing itself from transcendent metaphysics. Nevertheless, Gadamer is keen to stress the philosophical in philosophical hermeneutics. Reflection upon philosophical concerns, the life and death issues, the 'matters at issue' as Gadamer calls them, which draw us into dialogue and to which we endlessly return, are carried along by ordinary language. For this reason, Gadamer's hermeneutics is able to validate philosophical reflection whilst resisting the temptations of metaphysics.

Much analytic philosophy has, until recently, had a blind spot about history. History of philosophy was often conducted with little respect for the need for historical theory or more reflective self-understandings about what history of philosophy was for and what it was attempting to achieve.[3] This state of affairs is gradually changing as much recent analytic philosophy seeks to re-evaluate its own origins, but a more historical perspective on what analytic philosophy is and what it seeks to achieve would force it ever closer to a more hermeneutical style of philosophy. Gadamer would, no doubt, concur with the Hegelian sentiment, expressed in his *Lectures on the History of Philosophy*, that philosophy is the history of philosophy and the history of philosophy is philosophy. Although Gadamer states emphatically that he is not a historian of philosophy but a philosopher,[4] it is no stretch of the imagination to see *Truth and Method* as an extended dialogue with many of the key figures in the history of philosophy. Philosophical hermeneutics is able to overcome the division between philosophy and its history by showing how the two activities are actually part of a common enterprise. For hermeneutics, the history of philosophy is the fertile ground out of which grows contemporary philosophical questions.

Another piece of bridge-building relates to literature and the whole topic of figurative language. Philosophical hermeneutics is able to draw together traditional philosophy and literature in productive ways. In identifying the differences between analytic and continental philosophy, the topic of figurative language, and the inability or unwillingness of analytic philosophy to treat metaphor and tropic language generally, on a par with the proposition, is often mentioned.

This issue of the relationship between philosophy and the figurative no doubt goes back to the vexed question as to whether the philosophical enterprise is more like an art than a science. If philosophy is conceived as an art then literary language, metaphor and rhetoric are in order. Alternatively, if philosophy is viewed as having the full rigour of a hard science then the more literary devices are at best treated with caution and at worst excluded. Gadamer's hermeneutics tends to pass over this kind of dispute. He acknowledges that language in all its diversity, and this includes literature, metaphor and rhetoric, as part of the general strategy to achieve understanding.

It would be foolish to give Gadamer, like the devil, all the best tunes, for there is much that philosophical hermeneutics can learn from other areas of philosophical work and other traditions. But whatever hermeneutics needs to learn will, no doubt, be learnt if Gadamer's respect for dialogue and conversation, and his belief in the 'fusion of horizons', are taken to heart.

NOTES

1 See the discussion of utopias in the essay, 'What is practice?' (Gadamer, 1981), and in 'Practical philosophy' in Gadamer (2001).
2 Of course there is really only one tradition, the tradition of Western philosophy, for example, and the division into two traditions is inappropriate.
3 Programmes in the history of philosophy are integral to most academic courses of study in English-speaking institutions and yet there is little reflection upon the importance of that history. Why is philosophy studied historically with a narrative that starts with Thales of Miletus and generally ends these days with Michel Foucault or Jacques Derrida? There is every reason to study philosophy historically but some measure of historical theory or reflection upon the nature of the historical must surely accompany it.
4 When quizzed as to whether he was an interpreter of philosophical texts or a philosopher Gadamer responded emphatically: 'I may sometimes use texts, because I am unable to find the right words for a new vision. But I am not a historian of philosophy' (Rée, 1995, p. 29).

SUGGESTIONS FOR FURTHER READING

Gadamer's complete works are available in German in a 10-volume edition of the *Gesammelte Werke* (Gadamer, 1999). Most of his more substantial writings are now available in English translations. The revised second edition of *Truth and Method* is considered to be the most reliable translation (Gadamer, 1989). For the work after *Truth and Method*, the collection of essays *Philosophical Hermeneutics* is a very good supplement, expanding on many of the key ideas from *Truth and Method*. The main collection of essays on Gadamer's aesthetics is *The Relevance of the Beautiful* (Gadamer, 1986). The essay 'Gadamer's aesthetics' from the *Encyclopedia of Aesthetics* (Kelly, 1998, Volume 3, p. 267) is a helpful précis of Gadamer's basic position. On literature and especially his treatment of the lyric poem see Gerald Bruns's introductory essay[1] in *Gadamer on Celan* (Gadamer, 1997). Because dialogue and conversation are at the heart of Gadamer's work, the many interviews he gave in later life are good places to start if one actually wants to read Gadamer himself without reading his philosophical writings. He is at his most accessible in *Gadamer in Conversation: Reflections and Commentary* (Palmer, 2001), where his conversations with various interviewers range over autobiographical, personal and political reflections as well as offering insights into the philosophical work. Also useful is *A Century of Philosophy: A Conversation with Riccardo Dottori* (Gadamer, 2004).

For details about his life the autobiographical *Philosophical Apprenticeships* (Gadamer, 1985) is a useful and easily read work giving details of the major intellectual influences and friendships. Unfortunately, Gadamer himself is rather overshadowed by his teachers and friends and the reader does not really get close to Gadamer the person. The later autobiographical piece 'Reflections on My Philosophical Journey' (Hahn, 1997, pp. 3–63) again says little about the man Gadamer but is a revealing self-assessment of his own work.

Gadamer is at his most revealing and accessible in the informal setting of conversation and interview. Illuminating works in this genre are 'Interview with Hans-Georg Gadamer: Without poets there is no philosophy' (Rée, 1995), *Gadamer in Conversation* (Gadamer, 2001) and *A Century of Philosophy: A Conversation with Riccardo Dottori* (Gadamer, 2004).

The standard biography is Jean Grondin's *Hans-Georg Gadamer: A Biography* (Grondin, 2003). This is fairly uncritical of its subject but it is both scholarly and immensely readable succeeding to marry the life to the philosophy. Works critical of Gadamer's time during the period of the Third Reich are Orozco (1996) and Wolin (2000, 2003, 2004). Palmer (2002) defends Gadamer against the attacks from Wolin and Orozco. The most detailed and comprehensive bibliography of Gadamer's writings, even though it only goes up to 1996, five years before his death in 2001, is the one compiled by Richard Palmer in Hahn (1997).[2] A shorter version of Palmer's bibliography is Appendix B in *Gadamer in Conversation* (Gadamer, 2001).

For general background to the history of hermeneutics Palmer's *Hermeneutics* (Palmer, 1968), despite its age, is still something of a classic and an excellent introductory work. Other background works are Jean Grondin's *Sources of Hermeneutics* (Grondin, 1995) and his *Introduction to Philosophical Hermeneutics* (Grondin, 1991). Book-length studies of *Truth and Method* are few and far between. The best known are *Gadamer's Hermeneutics: A Reading of 'Truth and Method'* (Weinsheimer, 1985), and more recently *The Philosophy of Gadamer* (Grondin, 2003a). There are very few studies of the whole of Gadamer's work. Notable are *Gadamer: Hermeneutics, Tradition and Reason* (Warnke, 1987). The essay by Dennis J. Schmidt entitled simply 'Gadamer' in *A Companion to Continental Philosophy* (Critchley and Schroeder, 1998) is short but interesting. Jeff Malpas's entry on 'Gadamer' in the online *Stanford Encyclopedia of Philosophy* (Malpas, 2005) is well worth reading. The article itself is excellent and the bibliography is very useful with up-to-the-minute references.

Collections of essays on all areas of Gadamer's work are to be found in *Cambridge Companion to Gadamer* (Dostal, 2002) and *Gadamer's Century* (Malpas *et al.*, 2002).

More specialized collections include a series of essays on the problematical nature of truth in Gadamer (Wachterhauser, 1994) and a critical assessment of Gadamer in relation to his contemporaries in *Hermeneutics and Modern Philosophy* (Wachterhauser, 1986).

Too little attention in this present study has been given to Gadamer's influential interpretations of classical Greek philosophy. Especially worthy of note are his *Dialogue and Dialectic: Eight Hermeneutical Studies on Plato* (Gadamer, 1980a) – and *The Idea of the Good in Platonic-Aristotelian Philosophy* (Gadamer, 1986a).

NOTES

1 'The remembrance of language: An introduction to Gadamer's poetics', pp. 1–51.
2 'Bibliography of Hans-Georg Gadamer: A selected bibliography', pp. 556–602.

GLOSSARY

ANALYTIC PHILOSOPHY

Analytic philosophy, as a distinct movement in philosophy, is relatively recent but analysis as a philosophical activity is as old as the ancient Greeks. The key figures in the development of modern analysis are Bertrand Russell, Gottlob Frege and the early Ludwig Wittgenstein. Analytic philosophers tend to use the tools of logic and linguistic analysis to unmask the pretensions of metaphysics, and in this sense they are the inheritors of the empiricist thought of David Hume. Modern analytic philosophy focuses upon epistemology and the philosophy of mind and extends these to all aspects of traditional philosophy. Although there are some signs of rapprochement, analytic philosophy has been used as a label to identify those in the philosophical profession who show evident signs of hostility to what has relatively recently come to be known as Continental or European philosophy.

ANTI-FOUNDATIONALISM

Those who claim that knowledge cannot be grounded or given certain foundations are generally referred to as anti-foundationalists. Anti-foundationalists regard knowledge as a feature of something less solid and more contingent, say practical activity, or language or some other form of shifting agreements. This obviously contrasts with those foundationalist philosophers, like Descartes, who seek sure and certain foundations for knowledge and find them in experience or reason, that is, in the nature of the (knowing) subject.

CONTINENTAL (OR EUROPEAN) PHILOSOPHY

European philosophy, which is usually traced back to Immanuel Kant, integrates abstract philosophical reflection with more immediate questions about the everyday world, about the meaning of existence.

European philosophy, often allied more to imaginative literature than natural science for its inspiration, has spawned such modern movements as existentialism, phenomenology and hermeneutics, which are treated with a certain caution by some analytic philosophers. The criticisms of European philosophy from analytic philosophers are that there is too little regard for logic and the structure of argument and too much emphasis upon metaphysical speculation.

DASEIN

A technical term in the work of Heidegger often left untranslated but is equivalent to something like human existence:

> In everyday German language the word "Dasein" means life or existence. The noun is used by other German philosophers to denote the existence of any entity. However, Heidegger breaks the word down to its components 'Da' and 'Sein,' and gives to it a special meaning which is related to his answer to the question of who the human being is. He relates this question to the question of being. Dasein, that being which we ourselves are, is distinguished from all other beings by the fact that it makes issue of its own being. It stands out to being. As Da-sein, it is the site 'Da' for the disclosure of being 'Sein'. (*Internet Encyclopedia of Philosophy*)

DECONSTRUCTION

Although deconstruction is often taken to represent a method for interpreting literary texts, it was originally, as conceived by Jacques Derrida, an approach to philosophical texts. It aimed to show that such texts inevitably 'deconstructed' themselves, that is, they became victims of their own initial assumptions as they sought to repress or discount the inevitable alterity their philosophical terms depended upon. Part of Derrida's strategy of deconstruction was to illustrate the instability of literary and philosophical texts. In this endeavour he is very close to philosophical hermeneutics which also denies the possibilty of a definitive reading of a text.

EFFECTIVE HISTORY

Human understanding always takes place against a background of prior understanding and involvements and in this sense it is always historical. For Gadamer, the prior involvements are taken to be 'effective' because they have an effect upon present consciousness. Gadamer also speaks of *effective historical consciousness* to further bring out the sense in which consciousness is always in terms of the effects of the past upon the present. This does not make consciousness merely a reflection of the past because consciousness itself is operating upon the past.

ENLIGHTENMENT

From the seventeenth to the end of the eighteenth century was a period in European philosophy and ideas characterized by a variety of developments. The most important of these was the discovery of the procedures of natural science and their application to philosophy. In very general terms, the Enlightenment saw reason as the source of progress in thought and social life. In thought, it demonstrated the power of reason to challenge the authority of tradition. In social life it used reason to question the legitimacy of institutions, notably monarchy and the church. In recent years there has been talk of the 'Enlightenment project' by Alasdair MacIntyre and other contemporary philosophers. What these thinkers have in mind is a coherent programme. Using the ideas of the traditional Enlightenment thinkers there has been the suggestion that reason gives rise to optimism about progress and greater human control.

FUSION OF HORIZONS

A key term for Gadamer as it describes the activity of understanding. Each individual occupies a horizon and in attempting to understand another thing or person or text they extend their own horizon to embrace and 'fuse' with that of another. The image of fusing suggests that horizons come together and that understanding is seen to be more a question of (negotiated) agreement than the simple one-to-one relationship of a knowing subject to a known object.

HERMENEUTIC CIRCLE

The hermeneutic circle is an idea at the heart of hermeneutics. Most circles are to be avoided in philosophy but for hermeneutics understanding a text is always a process of bringing *part* and *whole* together in a way that can never be completed. In reading a book, for example, we always understand the immediate sentence we are reading at any one time in relation to the work as a whole. The idea of the hermeneutic circle is that the partial understanding of a bit of the text always modifies the whole and the whole the parts. The process of reading, understanding and interpretation is thus ceaseless; there is no one definitive reading of a text.

HERMENEUTICS

The word *hermeneutics* is a term derived from the Greek verb 'to interpret' and has two sources. One is from the Greek god Hermes in his role as messenger of the gods, while the other refers to hidden or secret knowledge. Originally the art of interpreting sacred, literary and legal texts, hermeneutics developed a series of practices and techniques for avoiding misunderstandings in difficult texts. Although Gadamer's work draws greatly upon the principal figures in the development of hermeneutics, his own philosophical hermeneutics is somewhat different. For Gadamer, understanding is hermeneutical. This means that the process of interpretation, as it applies to the reading of texts, say, is equally applicable to the practice of understanding.

HISTORICISM

This term has a variety of meanings. In its most obvious sense it is a philosophical position that attacks the idea that the structures of thought are independent of developmental and cultural factors. It works on the alternative assumption that all thought is ultimately historical because conditioned by its situation. This tendency emerges from the philosophical writings of Vico, Herder and Hegel. Hegel, for instance, sees truth not as a timeless given but something developing over the course of the unfolding of world history.

Historicists in this sense deny the possibility of timeless truth since truth itself is always to be understood within a particular historical context. Gadamer is a historicist in this first sense.

On the other hand, historicism can be understood to mean a form of historical thinking that is predictive. It builds on the past as a guide to developments in the future by understanding scientific-type laws of human development and using them in a predictive fashion. In this sense history is completely determined and by understanding the laws of historical development it is possible to predict the future course of history; this is the bad sense of historicism, criticized by Karl Popper in his essay 'The poverty of historicism'.

HORIZON

A term used by Friedrich Nietzsche and the phenomenologist Edmund Husserl to refer to a viewpoint or perspective. The term is taken over by Gadamer. He says: 'The horizon is the range of vision that includes everything that can be seen from a particular vantage point. Applying this to the thinking mind, we speak of narrowness of horizon, of the possible expansion of horizon, of the opening up of new horizons, and so forth' (*TM*, p. 302).

LOGIC OF QUESTION AND ANSWER

A term first formulated by the British philosopher and historian R. J. Collingwood. Castigating his contemporaries for ignoring the historical dimension to philosophical works he advocated a 'logic question and answer'. Every philosophical text, and presumably every argument within a text, is best seen as an answer to a question. Thus, as a reader trying to understand a text, one is constantly seeking to re-create (or Collingswood's term, 're-enact') the question the author sought to address and answer. This is an antidote to the unhistorical way of reading a text, which sees all propositions and arguments as part of a timeless logic of universal validity. Collingwood's approach sought to appreciate the historical context within which a text must always be placed. And although one could never penetrate the mind of the author one could at least see the philosophical text as an answer to a question the author had inherited or set himself/herself.

PHENOMENOLOGY

Phenomenology is defined as the study of the structure of consciousness. Rather than explaining consciousness in terms of philosophical theory, phenomenology puts to one side ('brackets out') theoretical assumptions and remains at the level of a first-hand description of the experience of consciousness. In this way it seeks to understand consciousness as it is lived and experienced. The founding father of modern phenomenology is Edmund Husserl, a pioneer of this procedure, although the term had been used earlier by G. W. F. Hegel in his *Phenomenology of Spirit*. The key figures in the phenomenological movement after Husserl are Heidegger, Sartre, Merleau-Ponty and others. Although Gadamer's early philosophical training encountered phenomenology by way of Heidegger it would be misleading to include him as a phenomenologist.

POSTMODERNISM

Postmodernism is one of those terms that defy easy definition as there are so many versions of what it actually is. The sense in which I have used it is to suggest that it is part of a body of opinion that challenges *modernism*; and *philosophical modernism* is just another way of expressing the 'Enlightenment project' as the period of the Enlightenment and the early modern age are roughly parallel. Postmodernism, whose hero is generally taken to be Friedrich Nietzsche, is an ironic, playful and sceptical response to modernism. Modernism, with its trust in the power of progress through reason and its allegiance to universal ethical and epistemological standards, is mocked by postmodernism.

TRADITION

The word tradition comes from the Latin *traditio* deriving from the verb *tradere*, which literally means to hand something over. So a tradition is literally what is handed over or handed on – or the process of handing on and handing over – from generation to generation. Traditions can be intellectual or practical. Concerning the former we might speak of 'the Western intellectual tradition' or 'the tradition of analytic philosophy'. Of the latter, one might speak of the traditional method of making baskets, for example. In the case of both the intellectual and the practical – and some philosophers would have a problem of teasing the one from the other – there is a handing down through the generations. (Perhaps worthy of note is the fact that *tradere* also means to deliver someone over, from which we get 'betrayal' and even 'treason' and 'traitor'.)

TRANSFORMATION INTO STRUCTURE

Gadamer's term to suggest that art transforms the everyday world not into an aesthetic dream world but another perspective on reality:

> Transformation into structure is not simply transposition into another world. Certainly the play takes place in another, closed world. But inasmuch as it is a structure, it is, so to speak, its own measure and measures itself by nothing outside it. Thus the action of a drama – in this respect it still entirely resembles the religious act – exists as something that rests absolutely within itself. It no longer permits of any comparison with reality as the secret measure of all verisimilitude. It is raised above all such comparisons – and hence also above the question of whether it is all real – because a superior truth speaks from it . . .
>
> The transformation [into structure] is a transformation into the true. It is not enchantment in the sense of a bewitchment that waits for the redeeming world that will transform things back to what they were; rather, it is itself redemption and transformation back into true being.
>
> In being presented in play, what is emerges. It produces and brings into light what is otherwise constantly hidden and withdrawn. (*TM*, p. 112)

BIBLIOGRAPHY

Baggini, J. and Stangroom, J. (eds). (2004). *Great Thinkers A–Z*, London: Continuum.

Bubner, R. (1981). *Modern German Philosophy*, Cambridge: Cambridge University Press.

Carnap, R. (1978). 'The overcoming of metaphysics through logical analysis', in M. Murray, (ed.) *Heidegger and Modern Philosophy*, New Haven, Connecticut: Yale University Press, pp. 23–34.

Collingwood, R. J. (1982). *An Autobiography*, Oxford: Oxford University Press.

Connolly, J. M. and Keutner, T. (eds). (1988). *Hermeneutics versus Science? Three German Views*, Notre Dame, Indiana: University of Notre Dame Press.

Craig, E. and Floridi, L. (eds). (1998). *Routledge Encyclopedia of Philosophy*, London: Routledge.

Critchley, S. and Schroeder, W. R. (eds). (1998). *A Companion to Continental Philosophy*, Oxford: Blackwell.

Davidson, D. (1984). *Inquiries into Truth and Interpretation*, Oxford: Oxford University Press.

Derrida, J. (2004). 'Uninterrupted dialogue: Between two infinities, the poem', *Research in Phenomenology*, 34, pp. 3–19.

Dostal, R. J. (ed). (2002). *The Cambridge Companion to Gadamer*, Cambridge: Cambridge University Press.

Eagleton, T. (1983). *Literary Theory: An Introduction*, Oxford: Basil Blackwell.

Forster, M. (2002). 'Friedrich Daniel Ernst Schleiermacher', *The Stanford Encyclopedia of Philosophy* (Winter edition), Edward N. Zalta (ed.), URL: http://plato.stanford.edu/archives/win2002/entries/schleiermacher/

Gadamer, H.-G. (1977). *Philosophical Hermeneutics*, Berkeley, California: University of California Press.

—— (1980a). *Dialogue and Dialectic: Eight Hermeneutical Studies on Plato*, New Haven, Connecticut: Yale University Press.

—— (1980b). 'The eminent text and its truth', *Bulletin Mid-Western Modern Language Association*, vol. 13(1), pp. 3–23.

—— (1981). *Reason in the Age of Science*, Cambridge, Massachusetts: MIT Press.

—— (1985a). *Philosophical Apprenticeships*, Cambridge, Massachusetts: MIT Press.

—— (1985b). *Philosophical Apprenticeships*, Cambridge, Massachusetts: MIT Press.

—— (1986a). *The Idea of the Good in Platonic–Aristotelian Philosophy*, New Haven, Connecticut: Yale University Press.

—— (1986b). *The Relevance of the Beautiful and Other Essays*, Cambridge: Cambridge University Press.

—— (1989). *Truth and Method* (2nd revised edition), revised translation by J. Weinsheimer and D. G. Marshall), London: Sheed & Ward.

—— (1994). *Heidegger's Ways*, Albany, New York: State University of New York Press.

—— (1996). *The Enigma of Health: The Art of Healing in a Scientific Age*, Cambridge: Polity Press.

—— (1997). *Gadamer on Celan*, Albany, New York: State University of New York Press.

—— (1999). *Gesammelte Werke*, 10 volumes, Stuttgart: UTB.

—— (2001). *Gadamer in Conversation: Reflections and Commentary*, New Haven, Connecticut: Yale University Press.

—— (2004). *A Century of Philosophy: A Conversation with Riccardo Dottori*, New York: Continuum.

Geras, N. (1995). *Solidarity in the Conversation of Humankind: The Ungroundable Liberalism of Richard Rorty*, London: Verso.

Grondin, J. (1994). *Introduction to Philosophical Hermeneutics*, New Haven, Connecticut: Yale University Press.

—— (1995). *Sources of Hermeneutics*, Albany, New York: State University of New York Press.

—— (2003a). *The Philosophy of Gadamer*, Chesham: Acumen.

—— (2003b). *Hans-Georg Gadamer: A Biography*, New Haven, Connecticut: Yale University Press.

—— (2004). 'Gadamer's hope', *Renascence*, summer.

Hahn, L. E. (ed.). (1997). *The Philosophy of Hans-Georg Gadamer*, Chicago, Illinois: Open Court.

Hirsch, E. D. (1967). *Validity in Interpretation*, New Haven, Connecticut: Yale University Press.

Hollinger, R. (ed.). (1985). *Hermeneutics and Praxis*, Notre Dame, Indiana: Notre Dame University Press.

Hoy, D. C. (1978). *The Critical Circle: Literature, History, and Philosophical Hermeneutics*, Berkeley, California: University of California Press.

Kelly, M. (ed). (1998). *Encyclopedia of Aesthetics*, 3 volumes, Oxford: Oxford University Press.

Krell, D. F. (ed.). (1978). *Martin Heidegger: Basic Writings*, London: Routledge.

Lawn, C. (2004). *Wittgenstein and Gadamer: Towards a Post-Analytic Philosophy of Language*, New York and London: Continuum.

Malpas, J., Arnswald, U. and Kertscher, J. (eds). (2002). *Gadamer's Century: Essays in Honor of Hans-Georg Gadamer*, Cambridge, Massachusetts: MIT Press.

Malpas, J. (2005). 'Hans-Georg Gadamer', *The Stanford Encyclopedia of Philosophy* (Fall Edition), Edward N. Zalta (ed.), URL: http://plato.stanford.edu/archives/fall2005/entries/gadamer/

Michelfelder, D. P. and Palmer, R. E. (eds). (1989). *Dialogue and Deconstruction: The Gadamer-Derrida Encounter*, New York: SUNY Press.

Misgeld, D. and Nicholson, G. (eds). (1992). *Hans-Georg Gadamer on Education, Poetry, and History: Applied Hermeneutics*, Albany, New York: State University of New York Press.

Moran, D. (2000). *Introduction to Phenomenology*, London: Routledge.

Mueller-Vollmer, K. (ed.). (1986). *The Hermeneutics Reader*, Oxford: Basil Blackwell.

Oakeshott, M. (1990). *The Voice of Liberal Learning: Michael Oakeshott on Education*, New Haven, Connecticut: Yale University Press.

Ormiston, G. L. and Schrift, A. D. (eds). (1990). *The Hermeneutic Tradition: from Ast to Ricoeur*, Albany, New York: State University of New York Press.

Orozco, T. (1996). 'The art of allusion: Hans-Georg Gadamer's interventions under National Socialism', *Radical Philosophy*, vol. 78, pp. 17–26.

Palmer, R. E. (1969). *Hermeneutics*, Evanston, Illinois: Northwestern University Press.

—— (2002). 'How Gadamer changed my life: A tribute', *Symposium*, vol. 6 (2), pp. 219–30.

Polt, R. (1999). *Heidegger: An Introduction*, London: UCL Press.

Rée, J. (1991). 'The vanity of historicism', *New Literary History*, vol. 22, pp. 961–83.

—— (1995). 'Without poets there is no philosophy: Interview with Hans-Georg Gadamer', *Radical Philosophy*, vol. 69, Jan./Feb., pp. 27–35.

Risser, J. (2002). 'Shared life', *Symposium*, vol. 6, no. 2, pp. 167–80.

Rorty, R. (1980). *Philosophy and the Mirror of Nature*, Oxford: Basil Blackwell.

—— (1989). *Contingency, Irony, and Solidarity*, Cambridge: Cambridge University Press.

—— (2000). 'Being that can be understood is language: On Hans-Georg Gadamer and the philosophical conversation', *London Review of Books*, vol. 22(6), pp. 23–5.

Scheibler, I. (2000). *Gadamer: Between Habermas and Heidegger*, Lanham, Maryland: Rowman & Littlefield.

Taylor, C. (1985). *Human Agency and Language: Philosophical Papers Volume 1*, Cambridge: Cambridge University Press.

Wachterhauser, B. R (ed.). (1986). *Hermeneutics and Modern Philosophy*, Albany, New York: State University of New York Press.

—— (ed). (1994). *Hermeneutics and Truth*, Evanston, Illinois: Northwestern University Press.

Warnke, G. (1987). *Gadamer: Hermeneutics, Tradition and Reason*, Cambridge: Polity Press.

Weinsheimer, J. (1985). *Gadamer's Hermeneutics: A Reading of 'Truth and Method'*, New Haven, Connecticut: Yale University Press.

—— (1991). *Philosophical Hermeneutics and Literary Theory*, New Haven, Connecticut: Yale University Press.

Wittgenstein, L. (1969). *Culture and Value*, Oxford: Basil Blackwell.

—— (2001). *Philosophical Investigations*, third revised edition, Oxford: Blackwell.

Wolin, R. (ed.). (1993). *The Heidegger Controversy: A Critical Reader*, Cambridge, Massachusetts: MIT Press.

—— (2000). 'Untruth and Method', *The New Republic*, 15 May, pp. 36–45.

—— (2003). 'Socratic Apology: A wonderful horrible life of Hans-Georg Gadamer', *BookForum*, Summer, URL: http://www.bookforum.com/archive/sum_03/wolin.html

—— (2004). *The Seduction of Unreason: The Intellectual Romance with Fascism from Nietzsche to Postmodernism*, Princeton, New Jersey: Princeton University Press.

INDEX